Pacing DAKOTA

Pacing
DAKOTA

THOMAS D. ISERN

From the prairies,

Tom I—

North Dakota State University Press
Dept. 2360, P.O. Box 6050, Fargo, ND 58108-6050
www.ndsupress.org

Library of Congress Control Number: 2018941181
ISBN: 978-1-946163-06-6

Cover design by Jamie Hohnadel Trosen
Interior design by Deb Tanner
Cover photo by Suzzanne Kelley
Map overlay in memory of George Amann
All interior photos by Thomas D. Isern

The publication of *Pacing Dakota* is made possible by the generous support of donors
to the NDSU Press Fund and the NDSU Press Endowment Fund, and other contributors to
NDSU Press.

For copyright permission, please contact Suzzanne Kelley at 701-231-6848 or
suzzanne.kelley@ndsu.edu.   .

David Bertolini, Director
Suzzanne Kelley, Editor in Chief
Zachary Vietz, Publicist Intern
Marie Wagar, Publishing Intern

Book Team for *Pacing Dakota*
Mike Bittner, Jack Hastings, Kirbie Sondreal, Amanda Watts

Printed in the USA

Publisher's Cataloging-In-Publication Data
(Prepared by The Donohue Group, Inc.)

Names: Isern, Thomas D. (Thomas Dean), 1952-
Title: Pacing Dakota / by Thomas D. Isern.
Description: First edition. | Fargo, ND : North Dakota State University
    Press, [2018] | Includes index.
Identifiers: ISBN 9781946163066
Subjects: LCSH: Great Plains--History. | Great Plains--Social life and
    customs. | North Dakota--History. | North Dakota--Social life and customs.
    | Isern, Thomas D. (Thomas Dean), 1952---Homes and haunts. | BISAC:
    HISTORY / United States / State & Local / Midwest (IA, IL, IN, KS, MI, MN,
    MO, ND, NE, OH, SD, WI) | BIOGRAPHY & AUTOBIOGRAPHY / Personal Memoirs. |
    BIOGRAPHY & AUTOBIOGRAPHY / Historical.
Classification: LCC F591 .I84 2018 | DDC 978--dc23

∞ This paper meets the requirements of ANSI/NISO Z39.48-1992
(Permanence of Paper).

North Dakota State University Press
Dept. 2360, P.O. Box 6050, Fargo, ND 58108-6050
www.ndsupress.org

To my mother, Marie,
who has crossed over to the other side
but remains curiously present as I write

TABLE OF CONTENTS

1. PROLOGUE

We made a drive around the farm, my elder brother and I. It was coming on autumn. Our ninety-eight-year-old mother had passed away in January, leaving her estate in our hands. It was time to settle things. Her instructions were, essentially, you two fellows work it out between yourselves. What sounds like a prescription for a family feud was, in fact, a perfect expression of the values of a German-American farm woman and the result of reasonable calculation on her part. My brother and I talked about wheat, feed grains, cattle, petroleum, water, quail, and deer. After ninety minutes the estate was settled, legal work to follow at its own pace.

Sometime during the night following — a night spent in the old hotel in town, now enjoying new life as a bed and breakfast — I was up in the silent dark. I settled into a corner of the parlor to do some reading and thinking.

I have a photograph of my great grandfather sitting in this exact place, he who, after years as a widower, took up with the widow woman who ran the hotel, married her, and lit his pipe in this corner of this very room. He then was about the age I am now. I hope that he, then, enjoyed the same sort of peace that I enjoy now.

So, that night, I did more thinking than reading. I did not have with me the collected works of William Stafford, but was able to recite to myself the most memorable stanzas from his poem, "The Farm on the Great Plains."

> A telephone line goes cold;
> birds tread it wherever it goes.
> A farm back of a great plain
> tugs an end of the line.

Stafford the poet calls home to the farm, but no one answers. Mother is not at home. Father is not at home. Finally the tenant answers, but he has nothing to say. The poem speaks of time, space, mortality, and resolve.

I am not tested in quite the way Stafford was in 1956, when he penned his poem. Our farm is still a going concern populated with kids, crops, and cattle. One of my life aims is to see the farm into the seventh generation, God willing. Still, Mother is not at home, Father is not at home. Or maybe they are. I do not think Stafford was Lutheran, but even he hints that home may not be merely terrestrial. As for me,

> My self will be the plain,
> wise as winter is gray,
> pure as cold posts go
> pacing toward what I know.

⊱─❖─◊─❖─⊰

What do I know? On a given day, punctuated with unimagined discoveries, I may think, not much. I tell my students all the time the most important thing you can learn is how much you do not know.

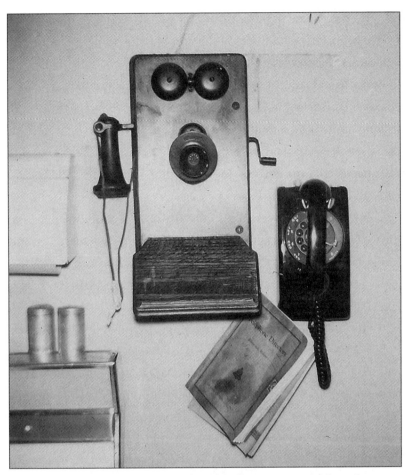

Wall telephones in the home place kitchen: our ring, three longs and two shorts

On another day, such as this one, spent reviewing work that spans decades, preparing this prologue, I think, well, I know quite a bit after all. There is evidence to that effect. Among all the compilations and publications, there is one line of work, unbroken, that strings the pieces together like beads. This is the work composed under the title Plains Folk.

In the course of more than forty years as a scholar and writer, I have been fortunate to enjoy the company of some splendid collaborators. Foremost among them: the sage of the Flint Hills, Jim Hoy, my friend and counsellor during my decade's service at Emporia State University, in Kansas. One evening in 1983, he and I were driving home from a joint speaking engagement when conversation disclosed we each had been percolating the same idea: a weekly newspaper column devoted to the folklife of the Great Plains. We decided to call it Plains Folk.

More than eighteen hundred 500-word columns downstream, the weekly feature still runs regularly in Kansas newspapers. Jim and I swap weeks writing it. Meanwhile, a whole lot of other stuff has happened, including my move up the map of the plains to Fargo, entering service at North Dakota State University.

In 2008 I entered into a congenial partnership with Prairie Public Broadcasting, now just known as Prairie Public, to put Plains Folk on the radio statewide in North Dakota. This meant I had to write, or got to write, many more features, often focusing specifically on life in the Flickertail State. I am continually delighted by the happy working relationship with producer Skip Wood at Prairie Public, while on-air hosts Merrill Piepkorn and Doug Hamilton have always framed my contributions in a way that is both kind to me and respectful of the regional culture described by my work. As the old joke goes, I do have a face for radio. As I travel the region, I am getting used to being recognized among strangers not on sight, but for my voice.

In my recounting of the course of Plains Folk over the years, I have deployed many metaphors. One day I call it a commonplace — recording passages, thoughts, and experiences in incremental fashion. Another day I think of it as a core sample, as might be lifted from a drill site by a geologist, that exhibits the depositions of the ages. I do not yet claim to reckon my own age in geological time; soon, however. For purposes of this book, Plains Folk is a quarry from which I have mined material to be laid into the edifice. I am both the miner and the mason. The stones are Plains Folk features written through the years that I have lived and worked in North Dakota. They are mostly about North Dakota, but they partake of a broader conception of the Great Plains as a continental region. The mortar is new material written to join the stones but also, I found as I worked, this material becomes substantial construction material in its own right.

At times, it appears in retrospect, I have crossed the red line into the territory of memoir. I hope the work remains, even in the realm of remembrance, the evident work of a scholar. It also is, perhaps foremost, the work of a plainsman.

I have lived all my life on the Great Plains of North America, Texas to Saskatchewan, except for brief times abroad studying the great grasslands of other countries. My grassy roots are in Kansas, where in Barton County lies the family farm, where at Emporia State University I won my spurs as a practicing historian, and where I nurture many tender ties. Since 1992, I have lived and labored in North Dakota, more specifically at the land grant university of the northern plains, North Dakota State University — an institution known to the rest of the country mainly for the heroics of its football teams (and I myself am a great Bison fan), but beloved to me for other attributes. Among which is one attribute that animates this book. Congress, in its wisdom in 1862 with passage of the Morrill Act, rejected the idea of a single agricultural academy situated in a central place. Instead, it deliberately decided to authorize an agricultural college in every state, every college to partake of the land and people of its particular place. A land grant university, descendant from an agricultural college spawned by the Morrill Act, is the right place for a scholar such as I am, dedicated to what I sometimes refer to as the regional project.

▷─◁▷─○─◁▷─◁

L iving a semi-public life, I get a fair number of semi-personal questions as I travel about the region, including the common query, are you retired yet? To which I reply, not hardly. Give me another twenty years.

Life has come to the point, however, where I have thoughts like: How many more Labrador retrievers are there in my life? How many F-150s? How many books?

Retirement, no. There is so much more work to do. See the family farm, as I mentioned before, into the seventh generation; see the grandkids through college; sign twenty dissertations; and through it all, advance the regional project, an enterprise in which I claim lineage and membership.

The regional project, as a vision for renewing the country (see Robert L. Dorman, *Revolt of the Provinces*), dates from the 1920s, when intellectuals in various provinces of the land self-consciously strove to root in the soil and channel the people of their particular places. They were scholars and artists who were of the people, were bona fide folk of the regions; who rose to prominence in matters artistic and intellectual; who were concerned about the state of the country; and who saw in its regions a source of vitality and character. Here on the prairies, then, think Willa Cather as novelist, Walter Prescott Webb as historian. Brilliant, blinkered, visionary, and sincere, they set the regional project in motion.

The University of Oklahoma Press, under the leadership of first Joseph A. Brandt and then Savoie Lottinville, established the importance of scholarly and trade publishing in order to anchor the regional project. Today, in the north, the North Dakota State University Press undertakes the same role, building the culture and sense of place with books.

I entered the realm of self-conscious regionalism when in 1979 I came to Emporia State, where the brilliant and cantankerous Patrick G. O'Brien had induced the Center for Great Plains Studies, a remarkable regional efflorescence. The regional project is like that — characterized by efflorescence, which emerges and recedes but never entirely disappears. When I departed Emporia State, I came to North Dakota State, home of the Institute for Regional Studies, the oldest regional studies center on the Great Plains of North America. So here I am.

Pacing Dakota.

2. THE GARDEN OF YESTERDAY

*Wherein the prairie historian removes himself to the archives
for edification and renewal*

In October 1871, Reverend Oscar Elmer, a native of New York and a graduate of the Union Theological Seminary, traveled from his previous station in Sauk Centre, Minnesota, to his new one in Moorhead, Minnesota. Sent by the Presbyterian Board of Home Missions to this border town where the Northern Pacific Railroad would cross the Red River into Fargo and Dakota Territory, Elmer expected to see a little of the wild west, and he was not disappointed. On the day of his arrival in Moorhead, the preacher wrote in his diary:

> Much excitement in M. A desperado, who had stolen $160 and robbed several parties was arrested. There was considerable talk of hanging but better counsels prevailed, about sundown he was clubbed out of town.

A few days later, Rev. Elmer did his first preaching in his new home. He described the meeting:

First Serv[ice] in M. felt slightly nervous. Held first
Serv. in M. in dining room of Chapin House at 3 P.M.
About 25 in attendance, among them a drunken man
who kneeled in prayer and gave responses. Evidently
thinking himself out of place he withdrew when I began
the sermon.

Elmer went on to organize congregations in Fargo, Grand
Forks, Casselton, Wheatland, Tower City, and Mapleton. He also
left behind a wonderful diary, which now reposes in the collections
of the Institute for Regional Studies, North Dakota State University
Archives.

Elmer was the classic western preacher, a cinematic sort of
character who labored hard for the Lord but was unabashed in his
fascination with the rough and rowdy ways of a sinful frontier. He
performed marriages for prostitutes trying to go straight, tried to
talk teamsters out of swearing at their animals, and preached to the
washed and the unwashed.

To make a point about Elmer's adventures on the ecclesiastical
frontier, we may note how he spent his first Christmas on the border. Here is Rev. Elmer's own written summary of that Christmas in
the Red River Valley, 1871.

Mercury 35 below at Moorhead. Rode home from
McVille starting at noon. The wind slight and in my
favor. Reached Holy Cross at twilight; drove across Red
River to Mrs. Fletchers whose husband was recently
frozen to death. When nearly there mistook the house
and leaving the beaten track, got lost in the drift at the
bank of the Wild Rice. Unharnessed and got out the
horse and started on much chilled. Mrs. F a Catholic
but with much culture and refinement, seemed grateful
for my call: urged me to remain the night. But about
9 o'clock with a bright moonlight started for home.

> The horse fatigued and the ride slow. Reached home about midnight. It is unnecessary to add that I was cold before I got a good fire. Yet with all this experience of cold and no dinner, I enjoyed Christmas especially in the satisfaction of giving sympathy and comfort to a bereaved person.

Open carriage, in the moonlight, -35°F. Merry Christmas, Reverend Elmer.

I hope it did not take too long for the good reverend to get a fire going and warm up on return to Moorhead that night, because reading his diaries, in the archives, I have become sort of fond of the guy.

As a professional historian, perhaps I should not admit that. Missionaries, you see, have a checkered reputation among historians. Not so long ago, until the 1970s, missionaries were generally considered to be good-hearted emissaries of civilization. Then historians changed their minds and decided that missionaries were agents of cultural aggression and sexual oppression. Now, as I say, it is a mixed review, because, particularly in dealing with native cultures, missionaries certainly were pushy and often were just wrongheaded. On the other hand, sometimes missionaries were the only whites who stood up for Indians when other whites were taking their lands. As for frontier preachers in white settlements, they have been caricatured by writers and moviemakers, but those caricatures commonly have come from writers who never inquired just what the frontier preachers said and did.

Which was remarkable, judging by Rev. Elmer's diaries. Dauntless, he strode into the saloons of Fargo to post notices and invite patrons to church services. He was willing to travel long, hard distances whenever his offices were called for.

In February 1872, for instance, he set out with horse and buggy to marry a couple in Grand Forks. The first night he reached

Georgetown, an outpost and stage stop where the Buffalo River entered the Red River. He enjoyed visiting that evening with representatives of the Hudson Bay Company, but remarked, "Less pleasant was the profanity of 'Swearing Jake Graham,' one of the stage drivers.

"I make it a study," wrote Rev. Elmer, "to reach these stage men . . . and win them from their profanity. Many of them are kind of heart but being away from the influences of house and society are very rough. . . . and tho' rough & reckless a closer acquaintance often uncovers a genuine vein of silver in their character moulded there, under God, by tender hearted praying mothers."

This preacher actually thought he could get stagecoach drivers to quit swearing! Worse, this chap Graham was "proverbial for profanity." The minister went to the barn to talk to him about it and found him there swearing at his horses. Rev. Elmer made some conversation, but decided it was futile to attempt any reform in Graham at this time.

The following night, though, the two met again at the next station north, where the Elm River entered the Red. Graham made it a point to carry water for the minister's horse, and then, reported Rev. Elmer, "At table he waited for me to return thanks and all the time I was there he refrained from oaths."

The rest of the journey to Grand Forks was perilous; pushing on to Goose River, Elmer recorded, "The roads were heavy [with snow], the horse weary, and those miles seemed to tantalize with their lengths. . . . the night shut down on me on account of darkening snow, like a huge bell." Fortunately, the pastor could make out telegraph poles to guide him in.

He went on not only to perform the scheduled wedding but also to preach the first church services in Grand Forks. En route back south he found the stagecoach stuck in snowdrifts, joined in efforts to free it, and noted that the hero of the day was an English dude whom everyone had considered of no account but who organized the work and did more than his share.

"All the mustaches in the party had icicles hanging to them one and two inches long," reported Rev. Elmer. "We were all in good spirits. . . . considerable grit was mustered in that snowbank. . . . This is the country to develop hidden resources."

So it was, and the missionary was developing a few of his own in the snows of Dakota Territory.

>─┼─◆>─0─<◆─┼─<

On June 6, 1872, Reverend Oscar Elmer noted in his diary that the first Northern Pacific locomotive had crossed into Dakota Territory by way of the bridge between Moorhead and Fargo. He underlined the passage, indicating he knew the symbolic importance of the crossing.

The progress of his own mission, however — promoting Christianity and respectability in the developing territory — was halting. A few days after the first train, the preacher agreed to marry Michael Gleason and Elizabeth Hohenbery, no fee to be charged. Hohenbery was a reforming prostitute, and the witness was "one of her female associates." Two days later, however, "Pimp Brownie of Brainerd" came to town, beat up Mrs. Gleason, and took her away.

The tendency of missionaries to be bigoted toward those not of their faith surfaced in the case of the local baker, John Gamble, who desired to marry a *Métis* girl — termed a "breed," or half breed, by Elmer. He managed to convince Gamble of the unsuitability of a match with a mixed-blood Catholic.

Rev. Elmer himself had a sweetheart in Minneapolis, whom he visited in April 1873. They had a pleasant time riding together, but it ended badly; they agreed not to correspond for the next year. Photographs depict the suitor as young, handsome, mustachioed, and animated, perhaps a good catch — but apparently the young lady was not interested in joining her beau in the wilds of Dakota. Elmer, nevertheless, located a homestead claim and hired some acres broken. One day, returning from work on the claim, he took satisfaction in a foot bath and, he recounted, had "a good time writing sermons."

It would have been easy for Elmer to be discouraged. Liquor was the biggest problem in the settlement. "My blood gets up over the liquor question," the preacher confessed. "See a drunken man pitched out of a saloon into the mud and also hear that a drunken half-breed had been carted down to the timber and tumbled out to lie exposed in the rain. Go to the Orleans Club, to Hansons & to Hennebokles" — all the notorious saloons — "and ventilate my feelings and warn them of the notice to all whiskey sellers to file bonds."

Still, there were rude joys and makeshift camaraderies to be treasured. On December 22, 1873, Rev. Elmer announced in his diary, "Someone has stolen the Christmas tree." Puckish settlers commenced making out bogus writs for the arrest of one another, until Jeremiah Chapin penned an equally bogus deathbed confession implicating himself along with four comrades in the theft. He confessed that they did "maliciously and willfully steal and purloin from the depot at Moorhead 3 tamarac[k] trees . . . said trees being intended for a Christmas festival to be held at Moorhead."

The following morning, five straw effigies appeared hanging from the railroad bridge. While Rev. Elmer went around collecting foodstuffs for the celebration and arranging the tree, which had been recovered, others ran an engine under the effigies and took them down gently. By Christmas, one had been laid out in a mock coffin, lined with muslin, in the depot. Wags put a wreath on it; marked it with the legend, "Body of J. B. Chapin, Salt Lake City Care of Brigham Young via Kittson Line"; and shipped it to St. Paul.

Rev. Elmer was in on the whole thing. However much he might exhort and rail against drinking and sin, he had become one of the boys in this territorial town. He had cast his lot with the developing frontier; the country was better for it, and so was he.

⊱┄◈┄○┄◈┄⊰

I rrespective of contents, the physical artifacts — these paperbound journals served up to me by kind archivists — are themselves intriguing. Distributed to farmers by International Harvester Company, their covers feature a red sun emblazoned "IHC" rising over a McCormick-Deering combine. Inside are forms where a farmer was to record daily activities and farm expenses. Tables at the back encourage calculation of the cost of horse and mule labor versus tractors — "Every farmer using horses or mules should know what they cost him," the text says pointedly.

Now I am reading the daily diary entries of Jules Emile Lebrun, a farmer near Milton, in northeastern North Dakota, and husband of Marie Pelletier Lebrun. And I am right in the middle of the horrible winter of 1936.

Early January finds Jules "choring around" the home place and sometimes heading for town or church in the "snowboat" — some form of motorized transport used when the roads are drifted shut, but I am not sure just what it is. He and Marie enjoy listening to the radio, its batteries charged by the windmill. The days are getting "cold and blustery," though, and several times Jules remarks he "feels pretty tough" because of colds and flu.

Now on February 4 the weather turns much worse — "Very very cold 42° below. 30 mile NW wind. Just sneaked out to barn and did chores."

February 8: "35° below. Bad blizzard all day. Did we burn coal and how!"

February 14: "Bitter cold. . . . Doesn't seem to be any hope that it will ever warm up. 3 eggs." Jules is counting down the production of the hens as temperatures drop.

February 15: "-52°! Getting worse instead of better. Stayed up till 1 AM to keep the fires going." No more mention of eggs.

February 16: "50° below again. Sure is awful. Coldest day in the buildings yet. High SW wind. Static on the radio. We're getting afraid of the elements by this time. Moved our kids in living room."

February 18: "No mail again doggone it! Looked out of the windows a thousand times but — just swirling snow."

What I hope to show by the passages above is that nothing so effectively transports one into history as a carefully written record inscribed by an ordinary person at the time the events happened. As I copied the passages I sat comfortably in the reading room of NDSU Archives, but I tell you, I started to shiver. It was a relief to read of the chickens starting to lay again on March 10, a comfort to see seeding begin on April 17, and an assurance to know the gophers were poisoned on April 22. God was still in heaven after all.

Jules Lebrun, a lifelong farmer, kept account books and farm diaries throughout the period 1930–1975. After he died in 1997 his sons, Richard and Bob, presented the diaries to the Institute for Regional Studies. They are absorbing reading, but they are more than that: because of their comprehensiveness and long span, they are the basis for detailed, scholarly study of what farm life was like in the middle of the twentieth century.

Thanks to the efforts of former archivist John Bye and the staff of the archives, priceless documents such as these came under excellent curatorial care and are made available to responsible researchers. Perhaps you know of similar records compiled by farm men and women across our region that should be placed in an appropriate repository to be pored over by nosy historians such as I.

►┼◆►─O─◄►┼◄

The story of Eileen Carl, later Eileen Tuff, as recorded in her diaries in the collections of the Institute for Regional Studies, NDSU Archives, confirms the old maxim about the sometimes rocky course of true love. Her romance with William Tuff, the two of them living near Denbigh, North Dakota, in 1906, took some hazardous turns.

Eileen's family must have been of modest circumstances, because she was working out as a hired girl on various farms. She had a beau, but her mother did not approve of him, although he had given her a ring. Eileen must not have been too enamored with him, either, because when she met William at the home of friends, she was smitten. She writes,

> I looked up to a tall dark haired grey eyed man and
> thought I had never see any man as hansom as he was.
> And I loved him in that very instant, and he afterwards
> told me the same thought came to him at the same
> time. Well we spent a very pleasant evening. He and his
> brother Johnnie played the violin for us and then we
> looked over some photographs and when Mary handed
> me Will's picture she said "That's him" and I thought, "it
> shure is," but of course I didn't say so.

Not long afterward Eileen writes, "On Saturday Will came in and we had a very serious talk and the next day when I went to Denbigh I was wearing a new engagement ring." She returned her previous beau's letters and ring. There was still her mother to deal with. Eileen writes, "Mother didn't approve of my getting married, but as I would be of age I told her I was going to wait until July and then we would be married. She never came to see me married and although I was disappointed I knew how she felt."

Evidently, too, the farm woman for whom Eileen was working at the time also was determined to sabotage the romance. Once Will came to see Eileen, who was out, and the woman wouldn't tell Will where Eileen was. Somehow the two lovers found one another and went for a ride together, but when Eileen got back to the house, there was a showdown. Eileen writes, "She started to tell me what I should do and what I shouldn't do and when she got through I told her a few things."

Eileen stayed after that with friends or with Will's family until they were married. She writes of her humble wedding arrangements, involving the cook car from a threshing outfit.

> I went back to Margie's and cleaned up the cook car and we had our wedding supper in it. . . . Then we went to Rugby and was married at the presterian Church then we went and had our pictures taken. . . . I was disappointed as Will did not give me a wedding ring but I had a beautiful engagement ring of one emeral and four pearls. . . . and if we are still living on our twenty fift anniversily I want a gold ring then.

The newlyweds took up housekeeping in good North Dakota style in their own dugout, a soddy built into a hillside of Will Tuff's homestead. The union would be blessed with twelve children. Nevertheless, Eileen would take an active interest in politics, and Will would serve in the North Dakota House and Senate.

>—·◆◇·◆◇—·◆◇·◇◆·—◆◇·◆—<

D akota Territory in the late nineteenth century was a place for a new start in life, so its legislators figured, and they wrote laws in line with that belief. Among these were the most liberal divorce laws in the country. Partly the laws were an expression of individual liberty; partly they were a matter of territorial development, making settlement here attractive to those desiring to escape from marriages back east; and there were other motives, too, which I will get around to later.

North Dakota and South Dakota inherited these divorce laws when they became states in 1889. Divorce here was quicker than anywhere else in the country, the two states imposing a mere ninety-day residency requirement prior to filing. Divorce-seekers flocked to the Dakotas, especially to the cities of Sioux Falls and Fargo.

Then in 1893 South Dakota increased its residency require-ment, which made Fargo, North Dakota, the divorce capital of America. This situation prevailed until 1899, when Bishop John Shanley galvanized moral reformers in the legislature to impose a one-year residency requirement.

In the meantime, the Cass County District Court was the leading divorce mill in America. Fargo had ready railroad connec-tions via the Northern Pacific; it had commodious hotels and good restaurants; and it had a battery of attorneys who were more than willing to serve any and all desiring to dissolve their vows.

Over a period of a couple of years I set a gang of bright stu-dents, the Senior Seminar in History at North Dakota State Univer-sity, to study this remarkable interlude in American social history. The records are ready and open, thanks to the staff of NDSU Ar-chives, which received them from the county.

Reading these records is an eye-opener. In the first place, there has prevailed among historians an interpretation of divorce in America that has emphasized changes in values as the cause of rising divorce rates. According to this line of thought, people in the 1880s and 1890s, the Victorian Era, read too many romance nov-els. Whereas previous generations had regarded marriage as a prac-tical matter, a covenant done to establish an economic unit and a child-rearing household, these Victorians believed in love. They had, historians say, "great expectations" of marriage. When their partners failed to be great lovers and devoted companions, they bailed out.

Well, the records tell many stories of expectations disap-pointed, but they are not expectations of the fluffy, romantic sort. The records tell of people who cheated on one another, abused one another, and simply refused to live with one another. Defying con-ventions of the time, men failed to provide, and women failed to make homes. All this stuff about true love, that was not the issue. Not great expectations, but minimal expectations, were the points of contention.

These cases are American tragedies, but there is also this whole other story more directly concerned with Fargo. To put it bluntly, people made bundles of money in the divorce industry. Hotels and restaurants flourished, newspapers prospered by publishing notices, and attorneys especially waxed fat on the nation's marital misery.

The students got into the papers, which were candid and most enlightening, of a Fargo attorney named Melvin A. Hildreth. Hildreth maintained an elaborate correspondence recruiting divorce-seekers from across the country, then catered to their every need once they arrived in Fargo. He wrote to a female client who had completed her ninety-day residency that she should come to his office and file her complaint, adding "and be sure to bring some money."

It was not the case, of course, that Fargo was some cesspool of immorality. It is just that for a few years there, much of the nation's marital misery flowed through this channel. It is not the stuff of a romance novel, but there is a heck of a soap opera in here.

One episode of which might be devoted to the story of Henry J. Losee. Like many of his fellow New Yorkers, whose home state had strict laws governing divorce, Losee came to Fargo, Dakota Territory, in 1885 to get a divorce. His wife, he contended, had deserted him. Taking the stand, he was asked by his attorney, "When did you first know that she intended to live separate and apart from you?"

"The first I knew anything about it," Losee declared, "was when I saw my goods on the dray going down the street."

The episode is no laughing matter, I suppose, but I cannot help myself, that is funny. This guy was down working at the shoe store near his home in Utica, and as he walks up the street, here comes his stuff piled in a wagon.

Not only that, he gets to his house to confront his wife, who he says has been content up to this point, and she will not speak to him. Seems his mother-in-law has arrived earlier in the day, and she informs him he has been treating his wife shabbily and she is coming home with her mother. Losee gets down on his knees and begs his wife to stay, the landlady his witness, but to no avail. So away to Fargo. Ninety days residence, a few more weeks for publication, and he is single again.

Next consider the case of Charles H. Potter of Cleveland, Ohio, filed August 9, 1895, in Fargo. He claimed his wife of twelve years had deserted him and, moreover, had treated him with "extreme cruelty," "caused him grievous mental suffering," and made "life in his chosen calling as an Evangelist subject to the sharpest criticism and disrespect, thus materially affecting his health."

Evidently he and his wife had an arrangement whereby he gave her twelve dollars a week, a business associate said, "for her personal expenses and pin money." Unfortunately, she was spending about a thousand dollars a year, running up debts all over town.

For the past five years Potter had been pursuing ardently his calling as a preacher, but his wife's desires were "contradictory and antagonistic." An acquaintance deposed, "She has been very fond of fashionable society and her associations and companionships have been all along that line with those who were inclined to dissipations and extremes." Worse, he observed her "during the race week in Cleveland on the porches of the clubs and at private dinners" and even saw her "drinking wine and upon one occasion in a company where some of the women were intoxicated."

The family nursemaid testified, "There was a coldness between them. . . . He was interested in Evangelical work, and very much devoted to it, while Mrs. Potter was fond of society." Enough, said Judge William McConnell. Divorce granted.

Reading these historic divorce files is about the snoopiest thing I have ever done as a scholar. I am thinking maybe these should be required reading for my students. Not so much for historical insight as for life lessons. Dibs on TV rights.

T he personal energy and historical passions of Myrtle Bemis Porterville were remarkable. Although born in Wisconsin in 1880, Myrtle Bemis grew up in Griggs County (Cooperstown the county seat), North Dakota. She taught in rural schools for a while before attending and graduating from Valley City Normal School. After another interlude teaching she went on to the University of North Dakota, attaining a master's degree in history in 1909—truly a remarkable achievement for the time. The next year she married Charles Albert Porterville, a farmer, and settled down with him back in Griggs County.

Only she never settled down. While Charles made his living farming and later in business, Myrtle threw herself into cultural and historical activities in Cooperstown and Griggs County. A historian through and through, she became an avid collector and writer. During the 1930s she collected and wrote for the Works Progress Administration (WPA). I am glad she did, because eventually her research materials found their way into the collections of the Institute for Regional Studies, North Dakota State University, and lodged at NDSU Archives.

It is amazing the things Myrtle Bemis Porterville accumulated. Obviously she operated with none of the constraints of liability, human subjects protection, or rights to privacy that bind archivists and researchers today. For instance, she collected some remarkable material on the drinking habits of her neighbors — during the days of legal prohibition.

I am talking about Box 8, Folder 2, of the Myrtle Bemis Porterville Collection, inscribed "Alcohol for medicinal purposes." Porterville went around to the pharmacies and somehow gained access to their prescription records. She copied down every prescription filled for alcohol, recording the date, the name of the thirsty patient, the type of alcohol administered, and the malady for which it had been prescribed. Her transcriptions comprise 388 prescriptions during the years 1905–1906.

So, who was doing the drinking? In the first place, as you might expect, almost all the recipients of alcohol were men. Of course, a man might obtain for a woman and vice versa, and sometimes prescriptions were recorded by initials only, but the overwhelming evidence here is that the men were the tipplers.

I expected Anglo-American surnames to predominate. I figured the doctors and pharmacists would be likely to prescribe for their friends in town. The surnames and addresses indicate this happened, but also that at least half the alcohol was going to Norwegian farmers — presumably good evangelical Lutherans! This indicates to me that the enterprise of issuing and filling prescriptions for alcohol was not any clubby affair, but rather a money-making proposition.

The prescriptions varied somewhat as to the form of alcohol to be administered. Most prescriptions were either for "alcohol" (grain alcohol, which could be doctored up in various ways) or for "whiskey." Some had more esoteric tastes. There was the occasional specification for "brandy" (one of these, "brandy for wife"), "gin," "port wine" (for "sacramental purposes," one insisted), or "sherry wine."

And just what sort of maladies, you may wonder, required the administration of alcohol for relief? Here is a list of things alcohol could cure: LaGrippe, influenza, "tight hoof on horse," swelling of man or beast (requiring lineament), confinement, colic, cramps, stomach trouble, dyspepsia, diarrhea, scalp disease, indigestion, cold, rheumatism, old age (I am not kidding, old age!), throat trouble, neuralgia, weakness, "female trouble," catarrh, asthma, headache, kidney trouble, backache, measles, "summer complaint," appendicitis, consumption, nervousness, and hay fever.

Does this not just set your imagination dancing? What sort of dialogues took place in the doctor's office, and after that in the drugstore? "More lineament, Mr. Erickson? Why, if I had a horse that went lame as often as yours does, I believe I would sell him."

Perhaps I am being overly suspicious.

Among the nearly nine feet of manuscript material in the Myrtle Bemis Porterville Collection is a modest item, the autograph book of one Russell Purinton, containing inscriptions from the years 1881–1895. This little clothbound book, 4 x 6 in., in landscape format, brown cover with gold print, is a reminder that nineteenth-century Dakotans lived in a different world, one where fountain pens recorded maxims and sentiments in a form that could be touched and savored.

The custom of keeping autograph books goes as far back as the sixteenth century. Some libraries today, such as the Mudd at Princeton University, hold large collections of them.

So here we have this little book compiled by a fellow named Russell Purinton, in which his friends, mentors, and acquaintances

Russell Purinton autograph book

left their marks. Quite a few of these, especially early ones, obviously came from elders, including teachers.

> In youth we ought industriously to occupy our minds in the attainment of useful knowledge.
>
> My dear young friend, Give respectful attention to, if you do not follow the advice of, those who are older.
>
> Remember thy Creator in the days of thy youth.

That last one is from Ecclesiastes 12:1, which points out the fact many of the inscriptions are not original.

> May there be just enough clouds in your sky,
> To make a beautiful sunset.

That one is a traditional Irish blessing. One of Purinton's friends left him a poem by Alexander Pope ("Like leaves on trees the life of man is found . . ."), another inscribed a passage from the 1700s by Thomas Gibbons ("Our lives are songs, God writes the words . . ."), and still another recorded a verse traditionally specific to autograph books:

> Within this book so pure and white,
> Let none but friends presume to write;
> And may each line by friendship given
> Direct the reader's thoughts to heaven.

The minority of writers simply wrote what was in their hearts. This from one of Purinton's mentors:

> I hope it may be my privilege to watch your course through life, for I feel sure you are going to make a noble man. Do not disappoint me. One of your teachers, and also your friend.

And this from a female friend:

> Do not forget the pleasant hours we have spent together.

Finally, I will add this remark about the common belief that the penmanship of earlier generations was a thing of beauty, in contrast to ours today: a flowing and beautiful script is not necessarily a legible one.

B rowsing the regional books in the archives reading room, I hit upon the works of James W. Foley, including a first edition of his book of poetry, published by a prominent New York house in 1916: *The Voices of Song*. In the front is one of those photographs protected by a tissue insert, with the bespectacled Mr. Foley peering out at us quizzically. Hair neatly parted and slicked, exhibiting a starched collar along with his coat and tie, he has come a long way since his rough and ready days in Medora, where his father had entertained that bookish and yet virile dude from New York named Roosevelt.

That same dude, writing from Sagamore Hill, contributes an introductory note to the book, recounting an anecdote wherein "the Foley boy" takes "a certain Eastern college professor" on a wagon excursion with an unruly team into the Badlands, with unfortunate results. As for the poet the Foley boy grew up to be, Roosevelt says, "as an old friend of the Little Missouri days I wish him well."

Mr. Foley was the poet laureate of North Dakota and the author of our state song, "The North Dakota Hymn." At the archives I have seen the original text of the song, handwritten on stationery of the Park Hotel, Watford City, North Dakota.

> North Dakota, North Dakota
> With thy prairies wide and free
> All thy sons and daughters love thee
> Fairest state from sea to sea.

Yes, this stuff is easy to parody, and from our perch here in the twenty-first century, we look back on Mr. Foley as a little bit of an embarrassment, his verse a rustic artifact of our bucolic past.

I am here to urge us all to think differently about Mr. Foley and to take another look at his poetry. In the first place, he was really a Bismarck boy. His mother kept the household in the capital city. Young James visited his father in Medora, then spent a year with him there after graduating from Bismarck High in 1888.

James became a newspaper reporter, starting with the *Bismarck Tribune*, and published popular works of poetry. He served as private secretary to Governor Louis B. Hanna. He loved North Dakota, and he loved his fellow man in a spirit of charity that perceived the better angels hovering over human foibles, even when those misadventures proved discouraging.

Studying clippings and manuscripts in the reading room, I learn that Mr. Foley ultimately left North Dakota for California, and did so with some distress. He evidently felt unappreciated in North Dakota, considered himself the object of jealousy and envy. Which is why his poem, "The Place that Is Home," is so poignant. He describes how whereas a sailor may be comfortable at sea, and a forest-dweller among the trees, a plainsman finds comfort only in prairie landscapes.

In my opinion, the greatest of all Foley poems is "The Garden of Yesterday." As preparation for reading it, google up the name Walter Benjamin, that Jewish martyr to Nazi tyranny who is adjudged a profound philosopher of history. I am not saying Mr. Foley was another Walter Benjamin, I am just saying he has a sense of the past redolent of that of Benjamin.

In "The Garden of Yesterday," the poet stands with a multitude of mourners gathered at the garden gate, excluded by Time, the gatekeeper, with whom they plead for access in order to search for what they have lost. Mr. Foley writes,

> All day I stood beside the gate from dawn to dusk, and
> saw them wait
> To plead with him to clear the way, that they might
> search in Yesterday
> But to them all he shook his head: "The way is forever
> closed," he said.

Mr. Foley knows how it is to stand at that gate; he knows what it is to be an expatriate; he sees, like Benjamin, the Angel of History. And that angel possesses not the charitable spirit of Mr. Foley. Mr. Foley thinks we should know that.

>–+–◆◇–◆–◇◆–+–◂

One brilliant autumn afternoon, having concluded that the deer hunting was hopeless, my hunting mate and I turned up a prairie trail west of Binford and followed it right to the top of one of those pyramidal hills characteristic of a terminal moraine. The view for 360 degrees was lovely. Directly north a half-mile rose another pyramid just like the one we were on, and in-between lay a perfect gem of a kettle lake, blue as blue can be, a few bluebills paddling around in the middle. Surrounded by such a striking landscape, I wished Daniel E. Willard could be there to expound upon it.

Back home at the archives I had been reading *The Story of the Prairies*, Willard's textbook on the landscape geology of North Dakota, first edition 1902. It went through another ten editions after that.

The book requires a little patience because Willard at times, despite his determination to communicate to the public the wonders of geomorphology, can be downright incomprehensible. Then again, he can be lucid and even inspirational.

A New Yorker by birth, Daniel Willard worked his way through to a master's degree in geology from the University of Chicago, then headed west to teach at the teachers college in Mayville, North Dakota, for eight years. After that he moved over to the agricultural college in Fargo for about the same period of years, before moving on to a career mainly in promotional work for railway companies.

Just before leaving Mayville, Willard published *The Story of the Prairies*, which is a fascinating snapshot of science at the turn of the twentieth century. Willard was mainly a field investigator, but he was a modern scientist, too. He felt the tension between scientific inquiry and social conservatism. As he discusses periods of glaciation, for instance, he declines to attach dates or years to them — thus avoiding conflict with fundamentalist conceptions as to the age of the earth. Only late in the book, in paragraphs buried deep in a chapter, does he address issues of geological time.

Willard's book is most fascinating in those sections wherein you can reconstruct and share in his travels, particularly as he explores the Badlands. I realize as I read that I am picturing Willard's landscapes as I know them, accessed by my Ford F-150, but everything looked different and unfolded more deliberately in the saddle, the way Willard saw things. Adjusting my perspective, I was able to share with Willard, having navigated the breaks of the Little Missouri, his joy on arrival at a humble log ranch house, "glad to rest and hear again the sound of a human voice," even though there was nothing to drink but warm river water, sediment-laden.

Driving home to modern readers the difference in perspective on the land wrought by mode of transport, Willard devotes the final section of his book to what he calls "Geology from a Car Window," by which he means a railroad passenger car window. He lays out a series of trip-logs following the Northern Pacific, Great Northern, and Soo Line railways across the state. It is an evening's amusement to get out a DeLorme atlas, or open up Google Earth, and trace Willard's extensive travels and lyric descriptions across the land. Better yet, take to the road, his book in hand, and follow Willard along the old railroad grades.

Get on Highway 13 between Lehr and Wishek, for instance, and enjoy the terminal morainic landscape of gleaming lakes and boulder-strewn hills that Willard first observed from the Soo Line, then examined horseback. "Majestic," he calls this landscape — not a clinical word of science, majestic, but the lyric expression of a poet.

Did Willard bring this poetic sensibility to the prairies, or did they instill it in him? I think he must have had it in the first place, but the land awakened it, as it will for any of us willing to invest our time and open our hearts.

▷─┼─◆─○─◇─┼─◁

"**M**y own people were pioneers," declares Bertha Rachael Palmer in her book, *Beauty Spots in North Dakota*. "North Dakota is my home state, the more I know about her the keener is my appreciation for her."

The book, published in 1928, is a work of patriotism on the part of Palmer. It is another gem in the collections of the Institute for Regional Studies. A member of the Daughters of the American Revolution, she dated her family roots back to the *Mayflower* and her personal story to a farm near Minnewaukan. She graduated from Devils Lake High School and, in 1903, from Mayville State Teachers College.

Palmer never married, as she was fully occupied with her professional and personal interests. She taught school for twenty years, served as deputy to State Superintendent of Public Instruction Minnie Nielson, and won election to that post herself in 1926. She served in that office until 1933, when she went to work as an educational officer of the Women's Christian Temperance Union. She wrote bulletins for the WCTU and traveled the country lecturing.

This makes it sound like Palmer might have been a stodgy spoilsport, but examining her WCTU bulletins, I find them gracefully written and lucidly argued. Palmer served the WCTU until 1959, the year of her death.

Her papers are held by the State Historical Society of North Dakota, where Gregory Camp has provided a fine biographical sketch of her.

So Palmer published *Beauty Spots of North Dakota* when she was State Superintendent of Public Instruction. She likely regarded it as an educational work. She was reacting against a popular attitude in North Dakota, where people seemed to adhere to a certain creed, which goes like this:

> We, the people of North Dakota, in order to see silvery streams and sparkling lakes, wooded slopes and shady dales, rolling hills, precipitous buttes and rocky canyons, shall at every opportunity hie ourselves to the broad expanses of Canada, the northern counties of Minnesota or the Black Hills of South Dakota, to insure to ourselves and our children, as we fly by in auto or railway train, brief glimpses of SCENERY for the enrichment of intellect and the broadening of experience.

"Popular opinion to the contrary notwithstanding," insists Palmer, "North Dakota contains wonderful and beautiful scenery, as majestic, as colorful, as fantastic and grotesque, as restful and peaceful, as glorious and inspiring as is found anywhere." Patriotism is good, and appreciation of your home state is good, but come on now, beauty spots in North Dakota, and scenery the equal of any to be found anywhere? Is this woman serious?

She is, and her argument makes sense when you consider what she is reacting against. The problem was what came to be known during the eighteenth and nineteenth centuries as the doctrine of the sublime, which sought edification in features of nature that were beyond beautiful, were spectacular to the point of extremity, even bizarre. Palmer is telling us, there is plenty of beauty near at hand, and any more is just overload.

I think of it this way. If you have an eye for beauty, then there is an infinite amount of it at any point of creation. If you lack beauty in your place, well, whose fault is that? So I am with Bertha Rachael Palmer on this, and I am looking for a good used copy of her book to grace my shelf. Besides which, it is obvious from her writing that she really got around North Dakota, and she asked people a lot of fool questions. I would carry her bags for a while.

T his curious notebook I am examining, bound in red and black leather, is identified on the cover with North Dakota Agricultural College (NDAC). Inside there are printed workbook pages and longhand pages of notes in black ink, the first ones jotted January 9, 1908, entries continuing to March 6. The writer of the notes was one William Adcock.

I heard from Margaret Olson of Valley City, who was working through some old effects, including this notebook of her father. She asked if there were an appropriate repository where it might go. I am happy to say that she subsequently donated the book to the archives of North Dakota State University.

When I picked it up at Mrs. Olson's apartment, she told me about the family. The parents of William Adcock, compiler of the notebook, were William and Margaret Adcock, immigrants from England. They had a farm south of Valley City. The son married the hired girl, Nora Munson, who came from a Norwegian family. Margaret, their daughter, finished high school in Valley and then worked for a hardware and auto parts firm in Fargo. In 1935 she married Bennie Olson, a teacher who subsequently became an automotive parts man in Valley.

Through this narrative run the threads of farm background and mechanical proclivity, which should have given some clues as to the nature of the notebook. Mrs. Olson said her father must have attended a winter short course at NDAC. Examining his notes, I find it was a particular type of course he completed: the certificate program for steam traction engineers. Young Adcock was an aspiring thresherman.

This makes sense, for NDAC was the best place in the country for such training, thanks to Professor P. S. Rose. He had come to the AC the previous year, a graduate of Michigan Agricultural College who had been working for a tool company. He would become a founding, charter member of the American Society of Agricultural Engineers and would serve as editor of important agricultural periodicals — first *American Thresherman and Gas Review,* later *Country Gentleman.*

He had the common touch, though. His 1962 obituary says he was "by nature a frontiersman," who at age eight in the Michigan forests, "took a man's place at one end of the crosscut saw, and at fourteen he was a seasoned ox teamster, log loader, and skidder." He had trouble getting into MAC because of inadequate school preparation. Thus at NDAC he had sympathy for chaps like William Adcock who were bright, ambitious, and mechanically inclined, but did not spell very well.

That winter of 1908, Rose taught the course for steam engineers. The following summer he offered the first such course for gas tractor operators. Things were in transition.

The president of the summer graduating class of tractor operators said in his oration, "We as engineers have and hold dangerous and responsible positions, not only for ourselves but for all others coming into contact with our labor in the field. Let us go forth determined to do our labor well."

Adcock's notes testify that such students did take their work seriously. Here are careful notes taken verbatim from the professor's maxims — I can see him pausing at the board, waiting for his charges to catch up in their note-taking. They took down complicated formulae for calculating pressure on metal and, getting to the heart of the matter, the "bursting pressure of a boiler." They also got little historical asides, such as, "George Westinghouse was the inventor of the Air Brake."

Some of the instruction was in the nature of fatherly, commonplace cautions. "Before crossing a bridge look at it and see that it is all right," Professor Rose admonished. "If the law says plank the bridge, plank it."

Another metaphor for life.

━╾━◈━○━◈━╼━

His own formal education amounted to only three months, but Haile Chisholm was the epitome of the educated man. He delighted equally in the forge and the lyceum. He was a great teacher because he was a great, lifelong learner. Haile Chisholm taught blacksmithing, and wrote poetry, at North Dakota Agricultural College.

Born in 1851 in Chazy, New York, Chisholm was held out of school on account of poor health, but oddly, began helping his father in his smithy. Subsequently he apprenticed with another smith, got a job in the locomotive shops of the Central Vermont Railway Company, and cast his first vote for Ulysses S. Grant in the election of 1872. He held several other jobs, started a family, settled for a while in South Dakota, and came to Fargo to work in the shops of the Northern Pacific Railway. In 1902, the year the NP shops moved to Dilworth, Chisholm became an instructor at NDAC, where he served until his retirement in 1937. This was a fortunate match.

Blacksmithing was a common study for students at the AC, and Chisholm's students remembered him as a teacher not only of skills but also of wisdom. Snorri Thorfinnson, who went on to a distinguished career in the extension service and as a local historian, wrote of Chisholm, "While I was not much of a hand at iron work, when I took work under you, I have always felt that I learned two lessons that stayed by me, the dignity of labor well done, and an appreciation of art."

Chisholm insisted that his iron work was no mere utilitarian pursuit but rather a matter of artistic fulfillment. He kept a commonplace book, that is, a book in which he wrote sayings and observations, which now reposes among his other papers at the Institute for Regional Studies, North Dakota State University Archives. Among the jottings of Chisholm is the statement, "I have never regretted a dollar spent for loveliness." Other commonplaces from the pen of Haile Chisholm:

> To sit idle when you feel that you should be doing something is the hardest thing in the world.
>
> Work is love made visible.
>
> Much time and money are spent for so-called higher education, but many recipients of this higher education never accomplish anything with it outside the drawingroom.

Chisholm believed that those who were inclined to be bookish needed to learn the dignity of labor with their hands. Those who worked with their hands needed to learn to regard their work as art and to appreciate poetry. Thus he had something to teach everyone, something he continued to learn himself all his life.

At lyceums and literary events on campus, there was Chisholm, and he had questions. Frequently he was called on to compose and recite poems to commemorate significant events at the college or at his church, First Methodist.

Among Chisholm's commissions of ironwork is the great gate that stood at the southeast entrance of the college and now has been restored to ornament that corner of the university. He also fashioned the ornamental gate that once stood in front of the Teddy Roosevelt cabin on the capitol grounds and the trowel used to lay the cornerstone of the capitol in 1932.

In 1931 the college faculty awarded Chisholm an honorary degree, Master of Artisans, saying, "He has elevated the art of craftsmanship in iron working to a fine art." He had to retire in 1937 on account of deafness, no doubt induced by his work at the forge. In 1941 the college community convened for a grand honorary dinner and for observances in the Little Country Theatre, upstairs in Old Main, where a quartet sang "The Anvil Chorus" — after which Chisholm and the others adjourned to attend the lyceum. After the death of his wife Mary in 1931, he lived with his daughter Anna until 1951, when the old smith died. Late in life he wrote,

I hear them say "He's passing fast,"
And what they say is true.
I'm not the man they used to know
In eighteen ninety-two.
'Twas not so very long ago
They called me hale and strong.
They found me ready night and day
To tote my load along.
My place beside the anvil true
I filled with honest pride;
My hands ne'er shrank from hardest tasks
By daily needs supplied.

If you listen to those stanzas, you can hear the hammer
in them.

⊱━◆◇◆━⊰

Through the course of this chapter's composition, I find my metaphors have migrated. Early on I borrowed the title, "The Garden
of Yesterday," from the poem by James W. Foley, because it seemed
fitting for the archival situation. I imagined myself laboring among
the shelves the same way I putter among the beds in my prairie garden. Now in the end I find myself drawn to the analogy of Haile
Chisholm at his forge. Indeed, overlooking my labors in the archives
from atop a bookcase, is a bust, a life mask in plaster, of the blacksmith Chisholm himself.

For a prairie farm boy such as I, the two metaphors are com-
patible. I will never sever myself from the soil; one of my life goals
is to see our family farm, dating from 1874, into the seventh generation. This persistence has required an inter-generational devotion to
hard work worthy of both the hammer and the pen of Chisholm.
For a prairie historian such as I, archives are both garden and forge.

They are a place for discovery and reflection, and thus renewal. They also are a place for sweat and tears, and thus satisfaction.

There is an ineffable potency in documents. They transport us, they grip our minds, they pierce our hearts. Historians do not need expensive laboratories or platoons of assistants. They only need archives, without which they are no longer iron from the forge, but mere sounding brass.

Bust of Haile Chisholm, smith and poet

3. A STORY THAT'S NEVER BEEN TOLD

*Wherein the prairie historian forsakes the dust of the archives
for the dust of the road*

Five pillars of sandstone mark the progress of a century-old vision across the southwestern corner of North Dakota. This was the Yellowstone Trail, a national highway in the days before there were national highways, the time when promoters dreamed them up and gave them grandiose names instead of uninspiring numbers. The Yellowstone Trail, they called it — Plymouth Rock to Puget Sound, its name intended to capitalize on a burgeoning tourist traffic to Yellowstone National Park.

The vision for the Yellowstone Trail came from a real estate promoter named J. W. Parmley, of Ipswich, South Dakota. Like others of his day, and especially others in the gumbo-cursed West River country, Parmley bemoaned the inadequacy of roads left to the maintenance of local farmers working out their road taxes. The dawning automotive age offered opportunity to those who would solve the problems of improvement of highways and navigation across the country.

Parmley seized the opportunity of a local good-roads meeting in Ipswich in 1912 to outline a scheme for what he called "a great transcontinental highway from ocean to ocean." The plan was to pull together road promoters from communities across the country, each to improve and mark its own stretch of road, and then promote the whole enterprise for the convenience of the traveling public. The road would be graded, but not surfaced.

Perhaps most important, the Yellowstone Trail would be clearly marked. "You don't need a log book," one brochure said. "Follow the Marks." The standard logo emblazoned on buildings and posts was a yellow circle around a directional arrow. Local collaborators, though, sometimes got creative.

The published history of Slope County details the arrival of the promoter, Parmley, in North Dakota.

> In 1913 a man by the name of James W. Parmley from Ipswich, South Dakota, came through part of Slope County with two mules and a wagon marking the proposed Yellowstone Trail for autos. He was painting sandstone rocks, fence posts, arrows around telephone poles, and other protrusions yellow to mark the trail. He would have one mule ride in the wagon while the other pulled, changing off while one mule rested.

The 1914 yearbook of the Yellowstone Trail Association depicts "Trail Day," designated as May 22, at Hettinger and Marmarth. As elsewhere across the country, farmers and businessmen turned out with teams, traction engines, picks, shovels, discs, graders, and improvised drags to transform boggy trails into a highway consisting of, the promotional literature optimistically said, "hardened earth." Parties of local ladies delivered picnic lunches.

At about this time a gang of fellows from White Butte, just across the line in South Dakota, quarried some limestone posts from a ridge on the North Dakota side and planted them along the trail as markers. I believe I know the exact site where they quarried

Mayor Sarah Chadwick with Yellowstone Trail marker, Haynes

the stone. For sure I know the current locations of five of these sandstone pillars that once guided travel on the Yellowstone Trail. Two are in Hettinger — one along Highway 12, the other on Main Street; one is in Bowman alongside the Pioneer Trails Regional Museum; one more is on Main Street of Gascoyne.

And the final Yellowstone Trail marker stands in its original location in the city park of Haynes. My companion and I spotted the yellow-painted post as we drove south along Main Street, as from the opposite direction came a little kid on a Hot Wheels bike. As we piled out of the truck with cameras and equipment, he took one look at us, made the turn west as directed by the trail marker, and spun gravel west and home to Mama, down the old Yellowstone Trail.

▸─◂▸─◦─◂▸─◂

Highway 12 angles across the southwest corner of North Dakota. It follows roughly the route of what was once the Yellowstone Trail, one of those named highways that crystallized during the 1910s and 1920s to promote cross-country travel. The Yellowstone Trail ran alongside the Milwaukee Railroad, which built through this country in 1907, spawning and linking towns like beads on a string. Some of them, like Hettinger, Bowman, and Scranton, remain vital today. Others, like Gascoyne and Reeder, are shadows of their former selves. Still others, like Buffalo Springs or Griffin, are just gone.

This southwest corner of the state is a historic landscape we have been rediscovering by following an auto tour laid out in 1938 by the WPA, the federal Works Progress Administration. It is Tour #9 as published by the WPA Federal Writers Project in its guide to the Flickertail State.

If you are following Tour #9 of the WPA guide, it says this as you begin your way northwest from the South Dakota border.

At 1 m. the route passes through a gravel area adjacent to HIDDEN WOOD CREEK, also called Flat Creek. Along its course, approximately a mile apart and covered with brush, are two cutbanks known as BRUSHY BANKS, near which the Custer Black Hills expedition camped on the way from Fort Abraham Lincoln in 1874.

On Hidden Wood Creek in this vicinity in 1882 was situated the main camp of the American Indians from the Standing Rock Reservation who took part in the last big buffalo hunt of the Lakota people, said to be the last large hunt in the United States, held under the direction of Major James McLaughlin, then Indian agent at Fort Yates.

Earlier this was, indeed, the campsite of Custer's Black Hills Expedition on August 8, 1874. With him were Dakota guides who led the column directly to this place, because they were familiar with it. The July 8 campsite on "Hiddenwood Creek" is clearly indicated on Custer's map appended to his expeditionary report. The WPA writers, I am pretty sure, misheard what to call the bluffs on the south side of Hiddenwood Creek. Local settlers called this site the Bushybank, not the Brushy Banks.

There is a lot to say about this historic site, but I am going to focus on some physical features and why they are the way they are. I do this on the basis of some specific historical evidence, including photos of the site taken by Custer's photographer, William H. Illingworth; a broader knowledge of the environmental history of the northern plains; and a bit of seat-of-the-pants reasoning.

The bluffs rising above the winding course of Hiddenwood Creek are covered with timber—not impressive forest, but good stands of chokecherry, ash, boxelder, and so on—as they were when Custer came. The creek always holds water here, even in droughty summers. Looking down from the heights, I see why: beaver dams. Beaver, of course, need the timber of the Bushybank as building material.

Now, why did this isolate stand of forest persist in a landscape that Custer otherwise labeled as sterile and barren? Why was it never consumed by fire? Hiddenwood Creek is too narrow to stop a prairie fire.

The forest remnant is no accident. In my opinion, what we have here is a forested enclave preserved through the centuries by native resident hunters who backfired the creek bottom in order to protect the Bushybank. Doing so, they could be assured of wood for campsites during autumn hunts. Moreover, the timber would keep the beaver at work on site, ensuring that traditional campsites for fall hunting also would have water.

And that is why Custer's Dakota guides knew just where to lead the expedition into camp on August 8, 1874. It turns out this trail is way older than Highway 12, the Yellowstone Trail, or the Milwaukee Railroad.

⊱⊱⊶⊙⊷⊰⊰

Listeners of my weekly feature, *Plains Folk*, on Prairie Public radio often ask how I keep coming up with topics. I explain that as a historical scholar, I am doing research all the time, and many scripts originate as spin-offs from larger projects. Other times I just get interested in a document, an artifact, or a conversation; do enough research to make five hundred words; pour myself a cup of coffee; and talk to the screen. When everything else fails, I conclude, there is always roadkill.

By which I mean I travel the Great Plains landscape a lot. The landscape is a library, and as I often say, there is a story up every section road. I do not approach the landscape as a blank photographic plate, of course. At my advanced age, including more than forty years as a professional historian, I am pretty well steeped in Great Plains history and lore. What I observe and learn from the people and places in the landscape often fits into my existing patterns of knowledge. Sometimes it causes me to reconsider what I think I know, to open my mind and think differently. Still other times it exposes me to experiences I never before saw or imagined. It is always worth talking about.

Some of the material is, indeed, like roadkill, unexpected stuff at the side of the highway. Often, however, I find things as the result of more purposeful exploration. The quest may be to find the battlefields of the Dakota War, or to locate the sites of German-Russian culture; to retrace the steps of a forgotten trail, or to identify the antiquities along a modern highway.

O n the coldest night of the year, following a season of exploration, it is comfort to sift through mementos of summer. At hand I have the photographs and field notes from hot days spent in southwestern North Dakota, retracing the auto tour laid out across the region by the Federal Writers Project in 1938. Here we are in the sun-bathed city park of Haynes.

Information in the tour guide about the town of Haynes is sparse: "HAYNES . . . was named for George B. Haynes, general passenger agent of the Milwaukee R.R. when it constructed its main line in 1907." This at least intimates Haynes was a railroad town, one of those little cities strung like beads on the tracks of the Milwaukee. It does not mention that Haynes was a marked turning point on the old Yellowstone Trail, forerunner of Highway 12.

Big open-range cattle outfits had occupied the territory in the 1880s, followed by smaller family operators in the 1890s. One of these, Mont Monroe, situated himself on Hiddenwood Creek, at the future site of Haynes, in 1899, followed by Joe Mischel, who settled just west of him in 1901.

A few years later — just ahead of, with, and in the wake of the railroad — homesteaders filled in the country, and the town of Haynes, originally called Gadsen, developed as a service town, with grain elevators on the south side of the tracks and Main Street stretching north. For a time it was a boom town, with three lumber-yards and two newspapers.

The high-water mark of the boom is the impressive brick-stuc-co school built at the north end of Main. It rose courtesy of a bond issue passed in 1917 by the optimistic voters, who saw a grand fu-ture in their town. As late as 1955 they passed another bond issue to build a gymnasium. Enrollment peaked three years later at 122. The high school closed in 1963, the grade school a decade later. A school reunion in 1973, however, registered 650 attendees, including peo-ple from both coasts.

The school today stands abandoned, a monument on its way to becoming a ruin, although the gymnasium alongside is kept up for storage of RVs and machinery.

The tour guide says nothing of all this, nor of the industrial establishment that built upon the original economic base of agricul-ture at Haynes. This was coal mining. In the 1930s, the tipple and loading facilities on the east side of town had to have been promi-nent, serving the producing mines situated in the hills to the north-east. Slag heaps and pilings remain today.

My field notes record gloomy impressions of Haynes — res-idences and businesses abandoned, mobile homes plunked down here and there — but also certain signs of life indicating that Haynes is not quite a ghost town after all. Such as Mayor Sarah Chadwick, personally mowing the city park, keeping things neat around the new generation of trees she herself planted.

In the middle of the park stands a remarkable monument, a bandstand built of petrified wood. A dated concrete block mortared into the petrified wood indicates a 1934 construction date. This pic-turesque semicircle, five feet high with taller turrets at each end, was piped for gas. My mind's eye looks over the shoulder of a musician playing a concert from a score yellow-lit by gaslights.

And over in the northeast corner of the park stands a yellow-painted pillar of sandstone, marking a turn for the old Yellowstone Trail, heading west for Hettinger.

Going through field notes and photographs gathered that summer, it is easy to become wistful. I think about strolling through the stone arch gateway into Mirror Lake Park, in Hettinger, North Dakota. Mirror Lake was the creation of the Milwaukee Railroad, which always needed water for its engines, and which also was the impetus for the founding of Hettinger in 1907.

Rudely crafted as it is — pillars of clinker rock mortared around iron pipe, with a steel girder supporting the rock stone arch — the archway nevertheless is a nicety, a laudable gesture toward dignity and beauty in a country town. It is to be noticed and appreciated, and I am sure it has a certain pleasing effect on people who pass under it, even if they never stop to think about it.

The legend on the arch reads, "In Memory of Hettinger Pioneer Businessmen's Club / A. O. Brown and M. P. Quickstad." A pioneer businessman's club. I imagine such a group getting together now and then in the manner of old settlers, reminiscing about the early days on Main Street.

If ever there was a pioneer businessman, it was Alfred O. Brown. The very first advertisement in the very first issue of Hettinger's *Adams County Record* announced: "A. O. Brown / Watchmaker and Jeweler / Located in Taylor's Barber Shop / All Work Guaranteed."

Born in 1883 in Minnesota, the son of parents from Trondheim, Norway, Brown epitomized the class of Norwegian businessmen typical of this frontier era on the northern plains. Second-generation Norwegians coming out of the midwestern states were the Yankee traders of the northwestern plains.

A course in watchmaking under his belt, young Brown filed on a homestead near as he could to the new railroad, which he would prove up while repairing watches and selling jewelry in town. In the meantime, when the business lots of Hettinger went on sale, Brown brought a plow in to the townsite and marked the lots with furrows so the bidders could see what they were buying.

Brown got active in local politics and community causes, even organized a dance band. He bought the bank in Bucyrus, built two rural telephone lines there, and stocked a ranch with shorthorns. Retiring from business in 1957, he organized the historical society in Hettinger.

Plenty of pioneering in that life, and likewise in that of Manvel P. "Quickie" Quickstad, pioneer grocer. Born in 1882 in Minnesota to Norwegian parents, he went west, worked in a grocery in Toronto, South Dakota, and then took up a homestead in Adams County, North Dakota—while also opening his own grocery store in Hettinger. There he married his hometown sweetheart, Florence, and they had two sons, both of whom went into business in Hettinger, and a daughter, who did not.

In fact, Shirley Mae Quickstad changed her name to Shirley Buchanan, went to Hollywood, had quite a few bit parts in film and television (one in an episode of *Perry Mason*), and married extremely well, more than once.

"In memory of," the arch reads. It serves, rather, to those of us unacquainted with the community, as an invitation to inquire, and to learn that there was such a thing as a whole class of Norwegian pioneer businessmen on the twentieth-century frontier of the northern plains.

⊱┈◦┈⊰

I t is possible you have seen one of these: an iron plate about twenty-four inches in diameter with the figure of a longhorn in the middle. Above and below the longhorn is the legend, "Going Up the Texas Chisholm Trail 1867." Near the bottom is a saddle astride what appears to be a chain of prickly pear pads. The whole thing was mounted on a post as a road sign.

The object in question was not a road sign on the old Chisholm cattle trail, although that might have been helpful at the time. It is, rather, a historical marker dreamed up and emplaced during the 1930s by a fellow named P. P. Ackley.

This fellow Ackley is said to have had some sort of involvement with cattle trailing, but his bona fides in that regard are unclear. One source says he was in Dodge City as a boy and trailed a herd up to Ogallala, Nebraska, in 1878, later serving as a brand inspector. Another says he was "an old-time Texas cowboy." Still another calls him a "southwestern cattleman."

The story of Ackley's Chisholm Trail markers even attracted the attention of the PBS television show, *The History Detectives*, which scarcely got to the bottom of the story, merely calling Ackley "a wealthy oil man." It appears, in fact, he was a stockman who lived in Elk City, Oklahoma, and owned property in the Texas Panhandle, from which he was fortunate enough to have natural gas royalties. A widower in the early 1930s, he was looking for a cause for personal fulfillment.

The Chisholm Trail, or rather its memory, became that cause. This was all well and good, except that Ackley had a liberal and ahistorical idea as to just what constituted the historic Chisholm Trail. In his mind any place cattle might have walked to on the prairies was part of the Chisholm Trail.

Members of the Old Time Trail Driver's Association protested that only the Indian Territory segment of the Texas-to-Abilene cattle trail rightly should be called the Chisholm Trail, but they lost that battle, as the public considered the whole trail properly so named. Ackley stretched the Chisholm Trail way south to Donna, in South Texas — evidently because he had a winter home there — and so one of his markers still stands there. Another stands in his home town of Elk City, which never was on the Chisholm Trail by any stretch of the imagination. It was on the Western Cattle Trail. Likewise an

Ackley Chisholm Trail marker was placed at Doan's Crossing of the Red River, also on the Western Trail.

The truth is, I do not know where all Ackley, who traveled around placing signs himself, put his Chisholm Trail markers. He talked about taking them all the way to Bismarck, North Dakota, and even into Canada. He might have planted one wherever he liked what he had for breakfast.

I know for sure he planted two of his Chisholm Trail markers in Scranton, North Dakota. One of them reposes now in the Pioneer Trails Regional Museum of Bowman, in fine shape, still commemorating the Chisholm Trail — six hundred miles away from any part of that historic cattle trail.

It is not for me, however, to make sport of the wistful commemorations emplaced by P. P. Ackley. We are more alike than I might care to admit in academic company. He and I, we both travel the Great Plains, meeting people and marveling at the landscape, asking fool questions, doing our best to invest the country with story. Stories are like trails; they show us the way.

‡

Windmills are matters of public policy and entrepreneurial enterprise today from Texas to Alberta. Wind generators have come to the plains in response to the national imperative for energy diversification. They constitute massive vertical intrusions on the level regional landscape. They are subjects of visible and vociferous debate. They are hard to miss.

Other sorts of windmills, once a pervasive element in the landscape and folklife of the plains, are vanishing. Farm and ranch folk as old as I or older recall the routine of windmilling—the endless round of checking and maintaining those wonderfully simple, and yet eternally cranky, machines. It was good for your vocabulary. Today the same round of pastures involves only the throwing of switches.

Most manufactured windmills have gone to junk piles. Collectors gather representative models into museum and private collections. We are not losing knowledge of this aspect of material culture; we are only losing its presence in the landscape. The bible for windmill collectors is *A Field Guide to North American Windmills*, by T. Lindsay Baker, who is the country's — probably the world's — foremost authority on historic windmills.

There is a family of farm and ranch windmills, however, that I fear is being lost not only from the landscape but also from memory. I am talking about homemade windmills, contraptions constructed of junk, imagination, and little or no money to catch wind and pump water for frugal citizens and their livestock. Once there were tens of thousands of them. Today I wonder if there remain dozens.

Back in the 1890s the homemade windmills of Nebraska were the object of fascinating studies by a man named Erwin Hinckley Barbour. Most of what we know about them, and the basic terms for describing them, we get from Barbour.

I have been fortunate enough to encounter a few homemade windmills, unused but still intact, in my travels over the plains. Near my native home in western Kansas I found one of the type that Barbour called a "go-devil." This consists of a square box on the ground, constructed of planks. An axle spans the top of the box. Arms and fans, looking like those on the rear end of a paddleboat, are attached to the axle. It turns, because while the top blades are struck by the wind, the bottom ones are blocked by the box. A Model T differential attached to the end of the axle converts rotary motion into reciprocal and pumps the well. This is the only go-devil windmill I have seen in the field.

I also have found two old windmills of the type that Barbour called the "merry-go-round." One of these is just south of Medina, North Dakota, and the other is right about on the Kansas-Oklahoma line, visible from Interstate 35.

Merry-go-round windmills turn around in a horizontal plane, like a merry-go-round. The ones that I have seen have cross-arms of wood, to which halves of oil drums are attached. They turn because the open side of the half-barrel catches wind, while the round side deflects it. The cross-arms turn a vertical shaft, and in each case, an automobile differential is used for the conversion of motion.

Old homemade, wooden windmills may go unnoticed. They are weathered, and most people would not see them for what they are. Those that remain ought to be noted and documented, as a remembrance of the inventiveness and spirit of past generations of plains folk.

I remember the day, coming home from a grouse-hunting expedition, I spotted a merry-go-round (MGR) windmill in North Dakota. There it was, a wonderfully jerry-built contraption on an abandoned farmstead, a little bit of folk genius few people today recognize. I was primed to recognize this feature of material culture, not only because I knew the historical literature, but also because, years earlier, I had encountered a dandy MGR windmill along Interstate 35 near Arkansas City, Kansas. That one was built from junk in 1937. Key parts were fifty-five-gallon oil drums cut in half lengthways, to serve as wind catchers, and the differential and rear axle of a Model T Ford.

This other old MGR windmill is similar, and it is located a few miles south of the Streeter, North Dakota, exit off Interstate 94. Six half-drums mounted on 2x2 arms sit atop a wooden tower and turn a vertical shaft. The shaft runs down to the differential salvaged from some vehicle — I could not identify it. The wheels on the rear axle protrude out to each side, and the north wheel is connected to a pitman. That converts circular to reciprocal motion and powers the pump.

The corner legs of the tower are 4x4s, with bracing of 2-inch lumber, and with a ladder of 1-inch lumber going up the east side.

The neighbors said, if I wanted to find out about it, call Herb Reister in Medina. It turned out the place was in an estate to which his wife, Esther, was a party along with her brother-in-law and sister-in-law. Esther and Herb gave me some background over the telephone.

This MGR windmill was built by Gottlieb Graf, who with his wife Emma (Stolz) Graf lived and kept a small herd of grade cows on the place. Wife and husband, although born in America, were both of German-Russian stock, and I suspect not inclined to throw money around frivolously. Hence Gottlieb's homemade windmill. Neither Esther nor Herb had an idea where he got the idea for the design, but MGRs were common in Nebraska a century ago, and this was the second one I found using oil drums and an automotive differential.

Gottlieb Graf died in about 1970, and the windmill has not been used since — although Herb says, "It would work to this day yet, if it was taken care of." Esther says it dates from her girlhood on the farm, but in order to date it more precisely, I would have to get someone to identify that differential for me.

※

Just where we were coming from, I do not remember, but I do recall riding through Hannaford, North Dakota, and saying, "Whoa, what's that, turn here!" "That" was a maze of signs, perhaps a fortress of signs, hand-lettered signs, in front of a residence on a side street but visible from the highway.

Signs with attitude: "Prepare to Meet Thy God," "Whoremongers and Adulterers God Will Judge," "God Is Angry with the Wicked Every Day," "He Hath Also Prepared for Him the Instruments of Death," "Fret Not Thyself Because of Evil Doers for They Shall Soon Be Cut Down Like the Grass," "Be Sure Your Sin Will Find You Out," "The Wicked Shall Be Turned into Hell," "There Shall Be Weeping and Wailing and Gnashing of Teeth," "All Liars Shall Have Their

Part in the Lake which Burneth with Fire and Brimstone." There are more, but you get the drift.

These are the signs, and now the wonders. I wonder who is so upset with his neighbors — and we can take the term "neighbor" in the broad, New Testament sense, I think. I wonder what the neighbors — and this time I am thinking literally, the people next door and across the street — what the neighbors are thinking. I wonder how someone becomes so disaffected as to erect a wall of statements as a barrier against something. I wonder, why in Hannaford, North Dakota?

There is a sign, too, I always wondered about in Fingal, North Dakota. Fingal has one of those main streets that make your heart ache, where old buildings speak volumes of human stories, but they speak mainly to empty streets. The creamery, the bank, and most of all that round-topped, false-fronted, white-stuccoed building at the east end, north side of the street, the one with the sign: "Starlite Garden" in sky-blue letters on a green background, and five yellow stars, punctuated with empty sockets for lightbulbs never replaced.

I was coming home from a fruitless fishing expedition on a hot summer day. A cold beverage in the Fingal bar seemed like a good idea, but I did not know what I was driving into. It was all-school reunion day in Fingal. I just missed the parade. The town was full of people, though, and that round-topped building was open for enjoyment.

It is, historically, a place of enjoyment: a dance hall with a ticket window in the foyer, a hardwood floor, and the music of memory. Today it houses the local American Legion post, along with all the trophies of Fingal's glory days — state tournaments, graduating classes with Buddy-Holly glasses and faith in the future.

Alongside the hall is an outdoor dance pavilion with a shell bandstand and a concrete dance pad. Starlite, starlight.

Across the street I got a beverage and started asking people about the Starlite. Oh yes, we're from Oriska, and when we were going together in the fifties, we came over every week. In those days it was big band music played by small bands. Then a few years later tastes bridged from swing to the beginnings of rock'n'roll, and people followed their favorite cover band, the Echo Men from Valley City, here to the Starlite, over to the town hall in Kathryn, and to many another lively venue in sleepy towns.

Was there ever a better name for a cover band than the Echo Men? I wonder if it is trademarked.

It was not what I was looking for. Nosy as I may be, I do not go around asking people to show me their legs (although in some cases, I might sneak a peek). I surely would not have asked this fellow.

Here is how it came about. I was following the auto tours laid out in the WPA guide to North Dakota published in 1938. Following a detour suggested by Tour #8, I drove to the town of Alice, eight miles south of the famous Buffalo Alice exit from I-94. Here, according to the guide, "At the Multz Cafe is a Collection of Indian Artifacts (open)." What has become of the Multz Cafe, I wondered, and its antiquarian collection?

Turning east onto Main Avenue I drove one block to the principal intersection, Main and 2nd. The northwest corner was a vacant lot. On the southwest corner was an architecturally mangled bank building with a corner entrance. On the southeast corner was the impressive Hartl Hall, a fine old community building. On the northeast corner was the less impressive After U Bar.

There are no Multzes in local directories. I walked around Alice with no clue where to look for the remains of the café. Following my standard field operations manual, then, I headed over to the After U Bar for accurate intelligence, or something like it.

Fortune smiled, and so did I under my muffler, as two old guys came out of the bar and took a lively interest in what I was doing walking around with a camera and GPS. Mention of the Multz Cafe provoked immediate and fond recollections of nickel cones dispensed by Lizzie Multz, the proprietress. She and husband Charlie operated the cafe in a building that stood just north of the remaining business buildings in Alice — across an alley, in what is now a grassy lot.

And what of the Indian artifacts? Both Multzes died, it seems, in the 1960s, childless. The café building was sold to a local farmer who moved it away. The artifacts were bought by a collector, and upon his death, were donated to the Bonanzaville museum of West Fargo. What we have here, I concluded, is the old familiar story of small-town decay and the sweeping of material culture into the central cities.

As I turned to go, the older guy remarked, "I figured you were going to ask me about my leg." So I did. He raised the cuff of his right overall leg to reveal a prosthetic leg of peculiar design: green plaid, bedecked with John Deere insignia, machines, and slogans — "Had it made for me over in Fargo." Here is a fellow who has not let diabetes destroy his sense of humor or his brand loyalty. I have a fine photo of this particular artifact, which in consideration of popular sensitivities I am not publishing, but if you stop by I will show it to you.

Rounding out a good day, I went up the road west looking for the Camp Sheardown historical marker, one of the many Daughters of the American Revolution monuments commemorating the Sibley expedition of 1863. Asking at farmsteads got me nowhere until I entered a yard with three dogs, two friendly and one not. Contemplating my options, I saw a big round bale coming around the barn and drove over to talk with the man behind the front-end loader.

He was large, friendly, and articulate, a breeder of Spanish mustangs for endurance races. He thought that as a historian I should have a couple such beasts. He had a braid down the back of his neck, a red bandana around his forehead, and a face ruddy from cold wind. He gave me good directions to the monument, a brass plaque on a boulder situated alongside a gravel road. The rifle pits mentioned in the WPA guide — well, you have to use your imagination, I suppose.

A good day ended with a good evening in a tavern inhabited by the perfect mix of customers that characterizes pub life in a healthy prairie town — young folks getting just a little out of line, old folks enjoying the spectacle, waitresses making good money for one night, ribs the special of the evening. No Indian artifacts. Perhaps a few wooden legs, I did not ask.

⊱─═◈═─⊰

Traffic gravitates to the two main highways across North Dakota, I-94 and Highway 2. Splitting the difference between them, though, is that lovely two-lane avenue, Highway 200. We spent a wonderful weekend messing around the western reaches of 200 and came home profoundly impressed with the forgotten heritage resources of the region.

The public is familiar with the Knife River Indian Villages, a National Park Service site, and now the Knife River Flint Quarries have been designated a national landmark, as well. Along the stretch of Highway 25 leading to 200, though, who bothers to turn off in Center and pay homage at the Hazel Miner monument? This odd little obelisk memorializing the girl who gave her own life to save her siblings in a blizzard is incised with a reference to Miscellaneous Record Book H in the office of the county recorder. There, on pages 130–31, we found the typewritten story of Hazel's martyrdom.

Even if travelers follow the trail of evidence about Hazel Miner, do they notice that odd little building with bars on the windows over in the corner of the courthouse square? It is a freestanding, brick county jail built in 1928.

All along and about Highway 200, nose around a little, and you find unexpected delights. In Zap stands an elegant community hall, and the town has a well-kept park alongside Spring Creek. "In about 1914 hardworking miners began digging coal from the North Dakota prairies surrounding Zap," says the bronze plaque on the gatepost, and it goes on to pay tribute to the historic and continuing labors of coal miners in the region.

In Golden Valley, if you divert a block south of the main drag, you may think you have crossed into a past generation, as there on the corner is the vintage Lindemann Standard station and garage. The attached garage is filled with a collection of historic motorcycles.

Take the road along Spring Creek, and you come to Golgotha Cemetery, resting place of the Lindemanns and lots of other Germans from Russia. The incised gravestone of John and Lydia Lindemann, depicting their journeys from the old country and the ships they sailed on, is a moving document of historical identity. Back in Golden Valley, the elegant Occident grain elevator is a monument of another kind.

Passing through Dodge, if you look south up Main, you have to follow your gaze up the hill to see the brick and glass-block 1922 school building. Park at the end of Main, and you climb a railed sidewalk up the hill to the front door. Alongside the walk stand delightfully naive concrete sculptures fashioned by students — a pronghorn with the horns gone and a grizzled frontiersman with a couple of fingers missing. A third statue, a bison, unfortunately was vandalized.

After lingering over these and other artifacts up and down Highway 200 and the Spring Creek valley, we ended up in Dunn Center for the annual cream can supper of the Dunn County Historical Museum. Visiting with Ed Darwin and other local historians there, we thought we were done exploring, when Clarence Schollmeyer offered to take us out to the family homestead and see the amazing buildings on it.

Clarence's Uncle Alfred told us how he worked with his father and brother to pour the homemade concrete blocks — ornamented with split glacial rock and colored glass — that were laid up into perfectly plumb walls.

To this magic stretch of Highway 200 we will return, physically as well as verbally. Come ride along with us.

▻─◆─○─◆─◅

When we take our field school students out to the Knife River Flint Quarries, the visit always begins with a madcap episode that makes them laugh out loud. I try to run ahead to get the pasture gate, sometimes successfully, and then Gail Lynch opens the throttle on her golf cart to lead the expedition up a mowed path into the quarries.

This time the hilarity was prolonged, for as we gathered around the golf cart for our orientation to the site, Gail was primed, and she launched into a monologue berating a certain state official who had failed to show up for the dedication of the Knife River Flint Quarries as a national landmark. This included not only a recounting of the episode but also a reenactment.

Gail is the sort of woman who, if you show up at her door, is likely to say, "What the hell are you doing here?" and then after that, "Well, I suppose you ought to have something to eat." I do not think I have to explain further.

The dedication of the flint quarries as a national landmark took place in June 2012, and was organized substantially by National Park Service staff at Knife River Indian Villages, working with Gail on arrangements. It attracted a fine crowd of neighbors and luminaries, and the spirit of the occasion was good. The designation as a national landmark had come through a year earlier, the culmination of a fairly long and deliberative process, the result of which was most pleasing to Gail and Allen Lynch.

Now Allen, he is a little different sort of character, and I will get back to that, after I fill you in on the facts about the Knife River Flint Quarries. The Lynch Ranch lies alongside Spring Creek, a tributary of the Knife River, just east of Dunn Center. The Lynch family acquired this property more than a half-century ago, not realizing what they had, just knowing that the land was so covered with big holes in the ground it could never be farmed. Active coal mines underneath it, too, had caused sinkholes, which attracted the attention of an archeologist, who quickly got more interested in the flint quarries than in the sinkholes. Subsequently Stan Ahler, then of the University of North Dakota, conducted significant excavations at nearby Lake Ilo, resulting in pretty good knowledge of the flint quarries, their significance, and their antiquity.

At least eleven thousand years ago natives commenced expeditions to this place to extract blocks of brown flint, which lay in the earth as glacial till. They excavated chunks of the stuff, carried them to nearby anvil stones, and fashioned them into rough blanks for transportation home, wherever home might be — for Knife River flint was prized throughout the middle of North America. I carry a shard of it myself in my pocket as a talisman and now and then pull it out to cut a beefsteak.

I do not mean to speak lightly of this, for the Lynch flint quarries constitute an archeological and historic site of the most profound significance that will be the source of pride and prestige to North Dakota for centuries to come. The Lynches, to their credit, are fully cognizant of this, and treasure the resource that history has placed into their hands.

Our visit always eventuates into the Artifact Room, which phrase, "Artifact Room," I encourage you to read in at least two ways and perhaps more. This is Allen's space in the house, where he gathers, broods upon, and grows mystic in the presence of his collections. Gail, you see, is not a brooder. She is an organizer, and she values the importance of the flint quarries to the community. Allen, he is transported by the artifacts and feels communion with their makers.

These are two different, and both wonderful, responses to the presence of antiquities at our feet. Antiquities need keepers, mystics need antiquities, and we are fortunate to have them all.

⋗⋅⊷⋅○⋅⊶⋅⋖

Q uickly now, tell me, is leafy spurge a perennial, an annual, a biennial, or a semi-annual? And can you name a breed of cow that produces a high volume of milk low in butterfat content?

I am reading to you from an examination in agriculture administered to seventh graders in North Dakota in 1958. Every student was to take the exam, with results to be compiled by county superintendents.

Before I go any further, the answers are, leafy spurge is a perennial, and the breed of cow is the Holstein.

At about the turn of the twentieth century, reformers in what was known as the Country Life Movement led the charge to insert agriculture as a subject of study in the public schools. This was important for the sake of practical knowledge, they said, but also for the sake of the prestige of farming. As you might expect, North Dakota joined in this cause and made agriculture prominent in school curriculum.

The printed, standard examination I am talking about is one I found in the one-room country school that sits alongside the Dunn County Historical Museum, in Dunn Center. I scored myself on it, and I did pretty well.

The exam comprises a set of multiple-choice questions about plants, both crops and weeds; a set of fill-in-the-blank questions about livestock; and a set of short-answer questions about farm economics. The farm economics questions are based on a reading selection describing a visit to the farm of Mr. Brown, who is quite a good farmer. He runs a diversified operation, implements sound conservation practices, and reads the circulars put out by the agricultural college.

The question I really like in this section is, "Why did Mr. Brown go to the Production Credit Bureau?" Does that not sound like a question that is going to lead to a good punchline? Why did Mr. Brown go to the PCA? Just try to say that with a straight face!

And then there is the most interesting part of the exam, a set of essay questions on "farm life," which I reproduce for you.

> How can we improve a farm so that it would be a more
>   pleasant place to live?
> How the city man is dependent on the farmer.
> How the farm of today differs from the pioneer farm.
> Why I like or do not like to live on a farm.

The question about how the farm today differs from pioneer times invokes the idea of progress. The one about how the city man is dependent on the farmer is resonant with farm fundamentalism. The other two questions go to the heart of what the Country Life Movement was about, that is, how can we keep our kids on the farm? In their own words, what do they like, or not like, about farm life? And how can we make the farm a place they will want to live?

I wonder in what attitude the county superintendents read the student essays on farm life. Were the essays read in a manner critical of the students, with the assumption they must be instructed in the right attitudes toward farm life? Or were they ever read in a manner critical of farm life itself, with the sense that what the students wrote might be actionable intelligence, that we might actually do something according to what they said? I would love to get hold of a set of these exams filled out by students in 1958. Surely they lie sleeping in a courthouse annex, somewhere.

>–+–+>–O–<+–+–<

Watford City, a remarkable town in transition, possesses a peculiar institution in its Long X Trading Post Visitor Center, which opened in 2004. As the name indicates, it provides information for visitors, as well as housing the exhibits of the Pioneer Museum of McKenzie County. It also is the location of the Watford City Community Benefit Association, which operates a package liquor operation for charity. The liquor store generates traffic for the museum exhibits.

The most popular exhibit is devoted to the last lynching in North Dakota, the hanging of Charles Bannon on January 29, 1931. This is a fairly gruesome exhibit, but in some ways it humanizes a twenty-two-year-old man who was the confessed murderer of a farm family of six, including an infant.

The Haven family, Albert and Lulia and their children, lived on a farm just north of the seat of McKenzie County, the town of Schafer. Schafer eventually lost the county seat to Watford City, which stands five miles to the west. Schafer today is a ghost town along Cherry Creek. The site has some interesting heritage buildings, including log structures, along with the well-preserved stone jailhouse from which Bannon was taken on the night of his demise.

The Havens were well-off, and Bannon was working as their hired hand. One morning in the middle of the milking he started shooting family members with a rifle, killing all of them and concealing the bodies. After this he just remained in residence on the farm, telling people he had rented it, and the Havens had gone to Oregon. Eventually his father, James Bannon, joined him on the farm.

Suspicions were aroused when the Bannons commenced selling off the Havens' possessions. This led to an arrest for larceny, to the discovery of human remains on the property, and to charges of murder.

Young Bannon made three confessions, none of which make much sense. His story was that he got into an argument with the

Haven boys, shot one of them, and then went on to kill everyone. It seems to me that train of events would have led Bannon to head for the hills in flight, rather than remain in residence. I suspect his actions were not random, but rather derived from a calculated plan to get hold of a nice farm.

For his actions, Bannon was taken from the jail by a large party of men and hanged from the bridge over Cherry Creek. His father was not lynched, but went on to serve a prison term. I have visited the jail in which the Bannons were held, and it is well-built, but the parties to the lynching were determined. None of them was ever charged for the lynching.

I have reflected, too, on the personal items of Charles Bannon and the artifacts of his lynching on exhibit in Watford City — the very rope with which he was hung, the death hood, a mask worn by one of the lynch party. A little notebook exhibits some written lines said to be a poem written by Bannon, but they are not. Bannon was not that literate. They are, rather, lines from "The Prisoner's Song," a mournful composition popularized by Vernon Dalhart. Dalhart sang, and Bannon wrote,

> Oh please meet me tonight in the moonlight
> Meet me tonight all alone
> For I have a sad story to tell you
> It's a story that's never been told

><+>+O+<+><

This has to be the best turtle yet. He makes Tommy the snowmobiling turtle in Bottineau look lightweight. He makes the We'el Turtle in Dunseith seem clunky. As big things go, Rusty the Turtle, alongside Highway 41 just north of Highway 200 at Turtle Lake, is just a great turtle.

I am getting more impressed with the Highway 200 corridor east-west across North Dakota every time I drive it. Work travel first familiarized me with the western reaches of the thoroughfare. That encouraged me to make more use of the eastern segment of 200 in crossing the state, resulting in encounters with many more charming communities and their appealing oddities.

Sykeston, for instance — what an evocative place, with its monumental brick high school, its footbridge across the lake, and the heritage buildings on Main Street—why, the ornate brickwork and stained glass windows of the old Citizens State Bank, those are just downright stirring. The heritage level of this little town is transporting.

Over in Hurdsfield, the very simplicity of the little green-and-white city hall and library makes me want to go in. I hope there are children still making use of this place, because its perfect lines and colors would have a good chance of imprinting a child for life as to the quiet pleasures of books. Surely this place must have a really kind part-time librarian, am I right?

Are you the sort of traveler whose expectations are met by such modest, genuine pleasures? If so, come on with me back to the highway, where the Dairy King is Hurdsfield's oasis on 200, and where creative spelling is a culinary art. I mean, I never saw anybody spell *Fleischkeugle* that way! There are two sizes — go for the big one, $6.50. Have some rhubarb-custard pie with it.

You want to stoke up if you are headed west, and then time your journey to hit Dodge at lunchtime, partly for the plate lunch that the Dodge Community Store will serve you, partly for the local color that gathers around the tables in the back.

Years ago I wrote about the Sons of Martha monument behind the Joseph Henry Taylor log cabin in Washburn, but I am still amazed at how little-known this fascinating piece of remembrance is. It reproduces the entirety of Rudyard Kipling's poem, "The Sons of Martha," which is a favorite of construction engineers all over the English-speaking world. Harry McLean, himself a great engineer, had the poetic monument emplaced in his old hometown.

Up the hill in Washburn, the Lewis & Clark Interpretive Center boasts the iron statues of Sheheke, Lewis, and Clark created by the welding artist Tom Neary, the same fellow who did the iron heart in McClusky and Rusty the Turtle in Turtle Lake—which is, perhaps I already mentioned, a really fine turtle.

⊱──◦──⊰

Public art is a risky business. Whenever a public authority attempts to make judgments on behalf of the people in matters of aesthetic taste, somebody is going to be unhappy, maybe even enraged. If the public authority making decisions is a distant federal agency, then you are just about certain to have controversy.

Lately I have looked into the dispute about the origins of the Indian mural in the New Rockford, North Dakota, post office — one of three federal post office murals in the state dating from the 1930s. (The other two North Dakota murals are *Rugby, the Geographical Center of North America* in Rugby, and *Indians Demanding Wagon Toll* in Langdon.) Background research on the subject reveals that communities up and down the Great Plains had controversies about post office art during this era. A good book telling this story is *Wall-to-Wall America: A Cultural History of Post-Office Murals in the Great Depression*, by Karal Ann Marling.

Federal officials kept trying to impose on local communities not only unfamiliar artistic styles and tastes but also interpretations of community history and life that were not acceptable. During the 1930s people on the plains got a little testy about how they were being depicted — *Grapes of Wrath* and all that. Sometimes they just outright rejected the art being thrust upon them.

In 1939 the Section of Fine Arts, which contracted with artists to do murals in post offices, conducted a special contest called the 48 States Competition, which meant to place a work of art in a post office in every state. A good idea, perhaps, but poorly executed. The works were supposed to depict local things and be designed with local advice.

So, a lovely mural of wheat shocks, or stooks, ended up in Flandreau, South Dakota. The only problem with it was that the artist, Matt Ziegler, did not intend it for this location. He was from Missouri, and so he painted capsheaves on the shocks. Plains folk hardly ever put capsheaves on their shocks.

Artist Philip von Saltza painted a mural called *Wild Horses by Moonlight* for the post office in Safford, Arizona. When the Section of Fine Arts moved the piece to Schuyler, Nebraska, he painted over the cacti in the mural and replaced them with poplars.

In Caldwell, Kansas, the postmaster, logically enough, wanted a herd of cattle coming up the Chisholm Trail. The artist assigned to the task, Kenneth Evett, kept trying to pass off other scenes. Eventually postal authorities intervened, and Caldwell got its cows. Anthony, Kansas, got a fetching wheat-harvest mural titled *Turning a Corner*, and Seneca got one called *Men and Wheat*, both of which satisfied local tastes.

The citizens of Purcell, Oklahoma, were fairly content with the bland pasture scene installed in their post office. They might not have been if they had known that the much better mural originally intended for Purcell, *Loading Cattle*, by James Baase Turnbull, had been hijacked and placed in Jackson, Missouri.

The biggest controversy, however, centered on Salina, Kansas. There, in 1941, artists Isobel Bate and Harold Black envisioned a great series of eight murals from Coronado and Juan Pedilla (yes, misspelled by the artist) to contemporary wheat fields. One depicted a farm woman looking over her shoulder at a tornado, her blouse open to the waist for no apparent reason. In general, citizens and the postmaster considered the murals "libelous" to Kansas, and so they were warehoused.

The paintings may not have been libelous, but like many of the post office murals, they were uninformed and inept. There is some kind of lesson about federalism in all this. And here is perhaps a final commentary. When we ask people in New Rockford about their post office mural, most of them say they never noticed they had one. I suspect it may be the same in Caldwell and Flandreau.

As for the mystery mural in New Rockford, the evidence is plain to see, but it is contradictory and confusing. It is right there on the wall, but it does not make sense. The mural is a striking work of art. Its official history is contained in a nomination of North Dakota post offices to the National Register of Historic Places in 1989. This document notes that three post offices built during the 1930s New Deal era are graced with murals done by artists funded by the federal government. In Langdon is the painting by Leo Beaulaurier depicting Indians confronting a wagon train scout. In Rugby is the mural by Kenneth Callahan featuring a map of the geographical center of North America with wheat and cattle scenes on either side. And in New Rockford is the mural, *Advance Guard of the West*, by Eduard Buk Ulreich. This is the mystery mural.

It is a mystery for several reasons. First, the title does not fit. The scene depicted is of a party of Dakota (so said Ulreich) warriors on horseback proceeding from right to left as you face the painting. The setting is shortgrass plains, with a buffalo skull in the foreground. The figures are highly stylized, somewhat reminiscent of flat style painting, but not quite. The title, *Advance Guard of the West*, connotes the advancing frontier of white settlement. These warriors appear to be, rather, the resistance to such settlement.

Moreover, I do not think the consultants who wrote the 1989 National Register nomination ever themselves viewed the New Rockford mural. They assert, on the basis of newspaper reports, that it was painted and installed by the artist Ulreich in 1939. Had they examined the painting, they would have noted a signature prominent on it: H. B. Bartron, 1961.

Now comes the grandson of H. B. Bartron, Don Bartron, himself an Oglala warrior and bundle keeper, a veteran Green Be-

New Rockford Post Office mural (with H. B. Bartron signature)

ret, to defend the honor of his itinerant artist grandfather. He says his grandfather Bartron, and not Ulreich, actually painted the mural in the 1930s and later returned to "touch it up" in 1961, hence the signature.

Years ago I wrote about this man Bartron and the murals he had painted in the café in Drake, North Dakota. I referred to him as a "hobo," which Don Bartron protests. The painter was not a hobo, but a traveling artist. He accompanied his wife, Blanche, a circuit teacher, where she went to teach, and painted in the same vicinities.

There is other documentation as to the relationship of the painter Ulreich to the New Rockford mural. He evidently made two preliminary drawings for the work. One, which has gone into the hands of a private collector, is substantially the scene painted in New Rockford. The other is quite different. It is a party of riders depicted in similar style, but they are cowboys, not Indians. This drawing now reposes in the Smithsonian.

So I am pretty sure Ulreich had the federal commission to do the mural. I am also pretty sure the one eventually installed in New Rockford was not supposed to be entitled *Advance Guard of the West*; that was to be the title of the cowboy mural, never executed. But what of the claims of Bartron and his grandson?

It is possible, it seems to me, that Ulreich, having made a preliminary drawing, subcontracted the actual painting work to Bartron, who was in the area. And here is another piece of interesting evidence: Don Bartron says he has in his possession the feather headdress worn by the central warrior in the mural.

Perhaps someone in New Rockford, not yet come forward, can shed some light on this. Perhaps people in other communities know of other paintings done by the itinerant H. B. Bartron. Otherwise, I am content to live with a few unsolved mysteries.

⊱⟶⊙⟵⊰

Sometime when you are passing through New Rockford, perhaps to check out the post office mural, turn off downtown and pay a visit to Hanson's Bar. It was built in 1913 by a druggist; the present bar was his soda fountain. A fellow named Irvin Anderson bought the building and converted it into a tavern in 1935. Its present owner and operator is Robert Lies, who has a loyal local following and enjoys lying to strangers, which is typical behavior for old tavern keepers. Look around the interior, however, and you will notice that the décor is not at all typical. The walls are filled with lush murals depicting western scenes. Lies produces a ladder and climbs up to locate the signature of the artist: Joe Breckenridge, 1947.

What can you tell me about this fellow Breckenridge, I ask? Lies says Cowboy Joe, as he came to be known, was a broken-down cowboy and a friend of his father-in-law, Irvin Hanson, former owner of the bar. Joe was a "small fellow" who painted big. Most of his paint he applied with a four-inch brush. It took him about a half hour to finish a mural. He was known across the country, even painting movie sets in Hollywood.

The Hanson's Bar murals are somewhat generic western scenes — blue lakes fringed by green pines, cowboys and campfires, horses and corrals, that sort of thing. There is a lighthearted humor in them. The only local identification in them is the legend, "Hanson's Bar," painted above a log building that never existed in life.

Who was this traveling barroom artist, Cowboy Joe Breckenridge? A newspaper clipping from Coeur d'Alene refers to him as Cowboy Joe, "the fastest painter in the world," a former rodeo cowboy from Montana who took up painting and could do a painting in three minutes.

There must be paintings by Cowboy Joe strewn across the country. There is a bar near Coeur d'Alene called the Snake Pit that displays, along with the obligatory deer heads, its own collection of Breckenridge paintings. Occasional pieces of his work show up in online sales outlets.

Most of his work is to be found in Washington and Idaho; he lived out his later years in Kootenai County, Idaho. A writer from Spokane says during the late 1960s he was a sort of "artist in residence" at Wild Bill's Frontier Saloon of Post Falls, Idaho. The same writer notes Joe was a Marine Corps veteran and had a considerable thirst (not that those two things go together). Joe boasted of appearing on the television show, *You Asked for It*, where he finished a painting in forty-two seconds. He died in Coeur d'Alene in 1972.

I have been in touch with a grand-nephew of Cowboy Joe, Mark Breckenridge, and a grand-niece, Rachel Garrett. They have kindly provided me with information about the family history and sent photos of a young Joe looking dashing, dressed in full cowboy regalia. Other parties have written me to report sightings of Cowboy Joe's work across western America.

It turns out, too, that there is another substantial set of his paintings here in North Dakota, seen by thousands of visitors every year, most of whom have no idea of their provenance. Hanging in the Old Town Hall Theater of Medora is a suite of Breckenridge paintings, some of which appear to be localized to depict badlands landscapes.

Is this great art? We do not need to convene extended deliberations on aesthetic authority to answer, no. Is it interesting and valuable art? That question I can, as a historian, answer easily. The Breckenridge paintings are documentation of a shadowy life in Western art yet to be reconstructed. We need more data points in order to see its full narrative arc. Every point that blinks into place tells us more about the emergence of the American West in popular culture at the grassroots.

Some say Cowboy Joe Breckenridge painted just to cover his bar tabs. Perhaps, but he also left a certain legacy, a body of work that we are talking about now. J. W. Parmley, P. P. Ackley, Gottlieb Graf, Gail Lynch, Tom Neary—in fact all the people, named or not, treated in this essay left marks on the land that anchor stories which otherwise would have blown away, leaving the landscape featureless. I find the features and tell the stories, to some satisfaction, if not much profit. So what is the point, other than conversation?

Conversation is the point. By the telling, I close ranks with all these characters to invest the land with story, make a place of it, a work that is never finished. I presume to be their interpreter, assigning value to what they have done. In this I am at least presumptuous, possibly delusional; I may not have a John Deere leg to stand on, but I think that eventually the conversation goes somewhere. From the countless stories, sources first of mere delight, come certain emergences, patterns that constitute understandings, maybe even a grain of wisdom. We should all live so long.

4. THE RESURRECTION AND THE LIFE

*Wherein the prairie historian confesses his faith in the
regions of the northern plains*

The dean of Great Plains historians, Walter Prescott Webb, famously defined the region with three adjectives: level, treeless, and subhumid. Those will do for an overview, I suppose, although they are uninviting. "Level" is fine with me; just do not confuse that with "flat." Could we, perhaps, instead of deploying the negative, "treeless," agree instead on the positive, "prairie"? As for "subhumid," who gets to say how much moisture is right, and how much is "sub"? I am thinking that twenty inches of rain in a year is about all the gray skies I care to endure.

Categorical adjectives also paper over the rich variety of landscapes and cultures comprised by the larger province of the Great Plains. Only strangers — some of whom live here — see sameness across the miles of prairie. We plains folk discern gradations, demarcations, and continual points of interest. Those of us who call ourselves farmers cannot resist appraisal of every locality we encounter.

I remember the time my mother flew up from Kansas to see me in North Dakota. She was accustomed to the prime farmlands and black soils of the Arkansas River Valley back home. Her first morning at my place in Cass County, she came along when I, as usual, took my Labrador retriever out on the section road for exercise. When we got to the corner, Mom swiveled around 360 degrees, looked at me, and adjudged, "This country lays real good, doesn't it?"

⸻

When people drive through the Red River Valley of the North, they do not see much. It is not a landscape that keeps travelers' noses pressed against the windows. Well now, what I just said is not exactly true. People look, but not intently, because they think they can see what is there with only a cursory glance, and after that it is just more of the same.

Even those of us rooted in the landscape and conversant in its history have, I would argue, the same drive-by mentality. We think we have it figured out: this is a landscape of industrial agriculture. We know this from our historians, from Hi Drache's book on bonanza farming and others. We know it from the section-range-township perfection of patterns on the land, right down to the perfect linear rows of beets and beans. An ordered landscape, the patterns of which are economic.

Then I spent some time studying a collection of my own photographs of the Red River Valley, from Pembina to Fairmount, and on closer look, another pattern emerged: the look of a landscape of faith.

That closer look, for instance, takes me through the doors and down the aisle of St. John Nepomucene Catholic Church to contemplate the Mucha of Pisek. The Bohemian and Moravian founders of this parish in Pisek, North Dakota, insisted that the faith of their fathers be transplanted into the new land, and they were willing to pay for it. Reportedly they sent some $1,000, a princely sum in the 1890s, to their Moravian kinsman in Paris, Alphonse Mucha, for a painting depicting the two founders of the faith in Moravia, Saints Cyril and Methodius.

Alphonse Mucha is known internationally as the originator of the school of decorative arts known as Art Nouveau. He himself considered his other line of work, the painting of epic scenes from Slavic history and culture, more important, and a finger of that line, the Mucha of Pisek, reaches into the Red River Valley. The Mucha is, I would argue, the most significant single work of visual art in North Dakota. You can view it on any day in the church in Pisek.

The Mucha of Pisek: Saints Cyril and Methodius

At the south end of the valley, in Fairmount, Father G. C. Bierens was concerned not with the planting of the pioneer faith but with its preservation in the modern times of the 1930s. Many Americans of those days were concerned about the supposed conflict between science and faith, but Father Bierens, who was also a bird bander for the United States Biological Survey, believed there was no such conflict. He believed rather that faith, properly construed, could accommodate or even subsume science.

The material evidence of Father Bierens's belief is the Sermon in Stone, a pair of striking obelisks standing alongside St. Anthony's Church. Embedded in them are all sorts of geological, paleontological, and archeological artifacts, along with religious symbols — crosses, keys, the Ten Commandments, the Alpha and the Omega. The Sermon in Stone stands to declare the landscape of faith to subsequent generations.

When I speak of the landscape of faith, though, I think most of all about Warsaw, North Dakota. If you are thinking I refer to the magnificent St. Stanislaus Church of Warsaw, you are only partly right. I also am thinking of the way that the Polish settlers of Warsaw extended their faith out from the church and into the countryside.

Across a township of territory around Warsaw are situated seven crosses erected at country crossroads. Polish farmers emplaced them in the pioneer landscape in emulation of the old country custom of wayside crosses. Farmers coming to town would pause at a cross to offer prayers. Families have maintained these wayside crosses over four generations and right down to present day.

For those who look and reflect, even for the driver of a quarter-million-dollar combine down one of these country roads, the wayside crosses of Warsaw still await prayers in the landscape of faith.

I remember when my companion and I went looking for wayside crosses, following a tip from the 1938 WPA guide to North Dakota. Making our way toward Warsaw, the Polish immigrant community in Walsh County, we knew there were some wonderful historical attractions in store. The centerpiece, of course, is the great red-brick church, St. Stanislaus, so stunning on the prairie horizon, and its interior so chock-full of wonderful religious art, including, of course, a magnificent stained glass window devoted to the patron saint of the Poles himself.

Not so well known are the fascinating cast iron grave markers in the cemetery, manufactured by Charles Andera, of Spillville, Iowa. One of them has that puzzling skull-and-crossbones motif on it, which I hope someone someday will be able to explain to me. These are fabulous artifacts under our noses. Around town, we discovered the family monument to Kiedrowski's store and the impressive old Warsaw Hall (since demolished, sad to say).

Then, in the countryside roundabout, we went looking for those crosses mentioned, tantalizingly, in the WPA guide to North Dakota, published in 1938. The guide reads,

> On ND 44 to the junction with a graveled road. In a triangle formed by the junction is a CRUCIFIX. On a base of natural boulders, in summer the clear, marble-like whiteness of the cross and canopied figure stands out in contrast with the green of the surrounding countryside.

That reference led us to a site just west of I-35 and a few miles east of Warsaw, where we found, sure enough, a crucifix atop a pole and a rough plaque on the pole reading,

WAYSIDE SHRINE / ERECTED BY PIONEER
POLISH IMMIGRANT LAWRENCE MOZINSKI IN
1910 / VINCENT & ISABEL GRANANSKI FAMILY
PAINTED & PLANTED FLOWERS / LATER YEARS,
EARL & LYDIA PLUTOWSKI FAMILY TOOK CARE
OF IT / IN 1969, BIG WIND TOPPLED THE CROSS
& BROKE IT / A NEW CROSS WAS ERECTED BY
ANTON & MARGARET MOZINSKI / CHILDREN

FLORIAN, STEVEN, HENRY, SARAH & FRANCES.
/ CURRENT CARE TAKERS WALLY EBERTOWSKI
AND GLORIA KOLTES / CHILDEN OF SARAH
WOZINSKI EBERTOWSKI / GRANDCHILDREN OF
ANTON WOZINSKI.

Reached by telephone, Wally Ebertowski confirmed that he was one of the family members taking care of the wayside cross, as they call it. By exploring the countryside, and also by talking further with Mr. Ebertowski, we came to learn there actually are seven wayside crosses arranged across a township of terrain surrounding Warsaw, each one erected early in the twentieth century and maintained ever since as a family tradition.

This is tradition transferred directly from the old country, as the erection of wayside crosses has both a long history and continued currency in Poland. Polish immigrant enclaves across North America have made their own wayside crosses, too. The complex of wayside crosses around Warsaw, North Dakota, is unknown outside the locality, but what a stunning display of prairie piety they constitute.

Mr. Ebertowski says, "A lot of people as they would go by, they would stop, some would pray, some just tip their hats." His father, he recalls, commonly would stop at a cross on the way to town and, ritually, "take off his hat and say a prayer." Of the cross under his care, he says, "I promised my mom we would maintain it."

It is not enough just to say, Oh, what a charming, old-country custom this is. Every one of these wayside crosses has a story; I want to know every one of them, and in time I will. Every such story, recorded and told, enriches us as people of the plains.

⊱──◆─○─◆──⊰

The crabtrees were flowering as we approached the Richland County Historical Museum, which stands alongside Chahinkapa Park, in Wahpeton. Across the street we checked out the 53 Counties monument, a plaque on which says it was dedicated in 1969 "to Robert J. Hughes, founder of Chahinkapa Park."

The plaque attached to the flagpole in front of the museum says it, too, is dedicated to "R. J. Hughes, founder of the North Dakota Auto Club, in recognition of his years of untiring service to the club and to his state."

A sign on the brick wall of the museum says it is a "Rosemeade Interpretive Center." It may be that the greatest achievement of the much-honored Wahpeton publisher Robert Hughes is that he brought Laura Taylor to Wahpeton to found Rosemeade Pottery. And, oh yes, he also married her.

Just inside the museum, above what is said to be the world's largest guestbook, hang portraits of Robert J. and Laura Taylor Hughes, founders of the Richland County Historical Society. Cases in the museum are filled with Rosemeade figurines, molds, designs, and other memorabilia of this highly collectible line of ceramics.

Laura Taylor grew up in Delamere, North Dakota, and attended Valley City State Teachers College and the University of North Dakota. After college she worked a while with the Dickinson Clay Products Company, which produced a line of pottery it called Dickota. Soon after, in 1936, Taylor was named to head up the WPA ceramics program in North Dakota, putting unemployed ceramicists to work.

Taylor and the WPA did some interesting work with North Dakota clay, but a crucial development occurred in 1939 when the WPA sent Taylor to the World's Fair to demonstrate her craft. It was there she met an attendee at the fair, Robert Hughes of the *Wahpeton Globe-Gazette*, who took a shine not only to the pottery but also to the potter.

Hughes persuaded Taylor to come to his hometown and found the Wahpeton Pottery Company, maker of Rosemeade ceramics.

Three years later the two were married. Another key figure, besides the hundreds of individuals who worked in the plant over the years, was Howard J. Lewis, who came in as plant manager in 1944. His particular contribution was the formulation of the distinctive glazes on Rosemeade pottery. Laura Taylor Hughes was the designer of Rosemeade products.

The cases at the Richland County Historical Museum are filled with examples of her work, including her signature pheasant figurines. Design sketches and plaster molds give a view of the creation process for these figurines so prized by collectors today. Personally, I want to acquire a pair of those bison bookends bearing the legend "NDAC" produced by Rosemeade in a limited run.

Laura Taylor Hughes died in 1959, the pottery factory closed in 1961, and the salesroom closed in 1964. Robert Hughes died in 1970.

Here is an intriguing mystery not fully run to ground. I believe that among the works Laura Taylor exhibited in New York in 1939 was the ceramic bust of Wilhelmina Geiszler, the martyr mother of the Germans from Russia, a bust made by Laura Hughes and now held by the McIntosh County Heritage Center in Ashley, the county seat. Back in Wahpeton, the Richland County Historical Museum exhibits a few other pottery items identified with the town of Ashley, in McIntosh County, indicating some sort of larger relationship with the community. My reading of the evidence is that the grande dame and community organizer of Ashley, Nina Farley Wishek, recruited Ms. Taylor to make the bust of Minnie Geiszler for the fifty-year jubilee of Ashley in 1938.

The bust of Wilhelmina Geiszler is one of the most historically significant works of art in North Dakota, not only because of its illustrious maker but also because of the story behind its heroic subject. That story takes us out of the valley and into German-Russian Country.

Bust of Wilhelmina Geiszler, by Laura Taylor, McIntosh County Heritage Center, Ashley

The Red River Valley is a part of the plains defined, fundamentally, by physiography. It is the bed of ancient Lake Agassiz, a farmland so rich you have to try hard to get a crop failure. Hence the valley's public image as a veritable factory of high-value agricultural product.

To the west lies the Missouri Coteau, a province of the prairies I have come to love dearly, partly because of having tramped so many miles across its pastoral hills, following a retrieving dog in search of sharp-tailed grouse. Then, too, in the course of my work I have gotten to know the ethnic immigrants who peopled the Coteau, most prominently the Germans from Russia — ethnic Germans who, after a century or so as invited settlers in the Russian Empire, emigrated next to North America. The progress of western American settlement in the 1870s and 1880s washed them up on the hills of the Coteau, where they dug in and remain today.

In recent years I have had the pleasure to meet and work with a cadre of people from Emmons, Logan, and McIntosh counties of North Dakota, talking about the potential for grassroots heritage tourism in this place we are calling German-Russian Country. With the rise of the independent traveler in twenty-first-century tourism, it becomes ever more possible to attract the sort of curious and sensible travelers we can welcome into our small towns.

By "independent traveler" I mean a person who is looking for real things in real places. Independent travelers scout their own itineraries, using the internet; travel by personal vehicle, rather than in large groups; and delight in finding interesting artifacts of regional culture on the ground. The culture of the Germans from Russia, including everything from religious sites to ethnic foodways, is of terrific potential interest to these travelers.

As part of the effort to promote German-Russian Country in a constructive way, I have been prowling the countryside, cataloging forgotten features of interest along with the obvious ones. Look up "German-Russian Country" in the online photo posting service Flickr and you will see images of many of the things I have been stalking.

For instance, at the south end of Main Avenue in the little town of Zeeland stands a compelling, inadvertent monument: the grand archway that once was the entrance to Zeeland Park. A century ago, and even during the Great Depression, Zeeland was a town of impressive vitality — including a formidable town baseball team that played in a fine ballpark, which is no more. Stand under the Zeeland Arch, though, and with a little help you can conjure the glory days of this prairie town.

While you are in the neighborhood, notice the Hilltop Cross that overlooks Highway 11 north of Zeeland. If you are passing at night you cannot help but notice it, because it is wired and internally lighted—red. It went up at the time of the bicentennial of the United States, and people refer to it as the Bicentennial Cross, but its message is more pious than patriotic.

German-Russian Country is, in fact, another landscape of faith, spangled with religious sites. There are the famous wrought iron-cross cemeteries, of course, but there are many other intriguing places of faith, more or less articulate, too. Just who, for instance, of the St. Anthony parish in Logan County decided to build the Pray for Peace Shrine along Highway 3 and ensconce Our Lady of Fatima, along with her plaster admirers, behind glass there? Certainly there is a link between the message of peace brought by the Blessed Virgin to those children in Portugal in 1917 and the sentiments of our ethnic Germans of North Dakota during the Great War.

The Germans from Russia, too, are inveterate agriculturalists, farming in their blood. Witness the folk monument emplaced along

Highway 34 east of Napoleon, which people have taken to calling the Dinosaurs of the Prairie. The children of Custer Grenz may have been exasperated by the old man's penchant for collecting threshing machines, but after his passing, the memorial they made was to arrange all the old machines on a prominent ridge and invite the public to reflect upon their German-Russian farm lineage.

We cannot neglect the distinctive cuisine of the Germans from Russia, in which dough in its many permutations figures so prominently, nor may we dodge the most controversial question of them all: just who, in German-Russian Country, makes and sells the best sausage? This I will leave open to perpetual argumentation and investigation. Man does not live by history alone.

⊳┤⊲⊳⚬⊲⊳┤⊲

One of the great resources for grassroots folklife on the northern plains is the local history collection of the Institute for Regional Studies at North Dakota State University Archives. I love that the shelves are open to users in the reading room, so you can pull down a dozen different centennial histories of this or that county and immerse yourself. The effect can be transporting. You begin to realize how profoundly different was the mentalité of prairie life a century ago. In the exploration of German-Russian folklife, as with most aspects of prairie lore, I find the admixture of fieldwork with library learning enriches both elements.

About this time in 1914, for instance, I read that citizens petitioned the Emmons County commissioners to place a bounty on gopher tails: 2 cents per tail in April or 1 cent per tail May through June 15. The commission agreed that gopher tails would be received by the county auditor, who would pay on lots of fifty only, after which he gave them to the building janitor to burn.

Kids would watch for the janitor to put the bags of tails into the incinerator, rake them out, and turn them in again. And again.

Stores in the county's towns took gopher tails in trade for penny candy. Storekeepers took turns taking the tails over to the courthouse in Linton. County employees hated this whole business. A photo in the Emmons County centennial history shows Judge Carley, Court Clerk Fogle, Treasurer Irwin, and Sheriff Kyes — all of them nearly hidden behind stacks of gopher tails, thousands of them.

That was just the beginning of the story, because a lot more happened off-camera, so to speak. I am sitting in the reading room trying not to disturb others by laughing out loud, thinking about all those Emmons County kids snaring gophers with twine, drowning them out with tank wagons from the threshing outfit, madly competing for pocket money, and then stealing their own tails back, or better yet someone else's, while the janitor is not looking, or maybe when he is looking; why should he care?

While we are laughing about old times, we should talk about the first football game ever played by the boys from Ashley, in 1921. They borrowed uniforms from the state normal school and took the train over to play Mandan, despite the fact that only one of them had ever even seen a football game played.

Local historian Adam Walker writes that after Mandan had scored a few touchdowns, one of the referees advised the Ashley boys they really ought to tackle somebody. Walker recalls specifically — because it was a rare and notable event — that Art Meidinger was the first to tackle one of the Mandan players, and he was quite pleased with himself.

Evidently the Ashley boys had a good time and were not discouraged by the final score of their first contest: Mandan 146, Ashley 0. In fact they went on to win their next game against Eureka Lutheran College, playing the game in blue overalls, with no pads. Having learned from the Mandan boys that cleats were helpful, they had gotten a local shoemaker to retrofit their shoes with cleats. They beat Kulm, too, sixty to nothing.

It only cost about three dollars to get the team kitted out with cleats. Which means, in those days, you could field a football team for the price of 150 gopher tails.

⊱—◦—⊰

The modest gravestone of Nina Farley Wishek, in the Ashley city cemetery, bears the simple legend, "Pioneer Mother." Perhaps that is enough, for Mrs. Wishek would have embraced both those labels, but what about "Author"? A teacher and a poet, Nina Farley Wishek is most remembered as the author of a remarkable book—*Along the Trails of Yesterday: A History of McIntosh County.*

I know what you are thinking, another musty old county history, but this one holds interest for people far beyond the confines of McIntosh County. For it records, in thoughtful fashion, the encounter of Anglo-American pioneers with North Dakota's largest ethnic group, the Germans from Russia.

Born in 1869, Nina Farley came to McIntosh County before statehood to homestead with her parents, from Michigan. She got herself a teaching certificate and taught in several country schools, including ones with German-Russian pupils. In 1891 she married John Wishek, a businessman who was German (not German-Russian) and who actively recruited German-Russian settlers to the region. So the two of them lived at the confluence of ethnic cultures. They are considered, historically, the founding family of Ashley.

Now, Germans from Russia can be a little sensitive about their ethnic identity, especially about stereotypes thereof, and so a book about their culture by an Anglo-American woman is a contentious proposition. There is indeed some rationale for taking offense, because a somewhat patronizing tone occasionally seeps into the narrative. Mrs. Wishek sometimes praises the stolid heroism of the German-Russian pioneers a little too forcefully, whereas at other times she speaks wistfully of the early Yankee settlers who departed, leaving the German-Russians locally dominant.

She includes one chapter entitled, "German Maids Whom I Have Known," meaning house servants, German-Russian country girls who came to town to keep house for Mrs. Wishek.

The titling of the chapter may have been a little insensitive, but it reflects a common historical reality. Throughout the Great Plains, Anglo-American townswomen recruited domestic servants from among the country folk, immigrant girls who entered such service to help their own families prove up and get established. This situation, so memorably described by Nebraska's Willa Cather in *My Antonia*, was not only common but also important. It was the way that Yankee families got to know the immigrant cultures of the countryside.

In this case, Mrs. Wishek got to know the country girls not just incidentally but also by insistently questioning them about their family histories, including life in the old country and immigration to North Dakota. "Often girls came into my home who had been over from the old country only a week or two," writes Wishek. "As time passed and I became more conversant with the German tongue, I learned more of the Old World and the way in which they lived there." She tells some of their stories, including one of a family traumatically divided by a case of trachoma, which caused a sister of the maid telling the tale to be turned back at Ellis Island.

The sister eventually made it to America, however, and became another in Mrs. Wishek's series of German-Russian maids. "Today she lives in Ashley, highly respected and greatly loved by relatives and friends," her chronicler concludes.

We are left with this poignant narrative of cultural exchange, a book worth reading before an expedition into German-Russian Country, and then again after.

I have a love story to tell you in two parts, both of them legendary.

The first part focuses on a woman hailed by historian Nina Farley Wishek as "the Heroine of the Prairie," but whom I have always referred to as "the Martyr Mother of the German-Russians." Wilhelmina "Minnie" Bauer Geiszler married her husband John in the southern part of Dakota Territory in 1885. Both of them were Germans recently arrived from Russia. The newlyweds pushed on to McIntosh County, where they homesteaded and started a family, which grew to comprise eight children.

One afternoon in April 1898, Minnie was keeping house, John was plowing, and two of their daughters, Mary and Anna, went out to fetch the cows. They all observed a prairie fire bearing down from the northwest. As John headed home, Minnie went after the two girls, who themselves showed good sense in the face of crisis. Each grabbed a cow's tail and was pulled along at good speed back toward the house.

Mary made it through the fireguard to safety. Anna stepped in a gopher hole, and the fire swept over her. Minnie raced through the fire, getting terribly burned herself, and tried to save Anna by pulling off the child's burning clothing and covering her with her apron. Her efforts were in vain, for Anna died two days later. Minnie lingered, suffering, but succumbed after two weeks.

Later in the year John Geiszler remarried, to a woman with whom he had thirteen more children. Indeed, Mr. Geiszler would have five wives before dying in 1948.

Doubtless they all were saints, but Minnie is the one who is memorialized, I suspect through the efforts of Nina Wishek. At the time of Ashley's Golden Jubilee in 1938, someone, probably the redoubtable Mrs. Wishek, as I earlier mentioned, recalled the tragic story of Minnie Geiszler and arranged to have a ceramic bust made in her likeness. Which brings us to the second part of our love story.

The sculptor of the bust, of course, was Laura Taylor, art graduate of the University of North Dakota, director of North Dakota's

WPA Ceramics Program, headquartered in Mandan. Her romance with Wahpeton businessman Robert Hughes is our second love story, connecting German-Russian Country with the Red River Valley.

The trade name of their ceramics company, Rosemeade, will resonate with any antiquarian reading this account. Rosemeade figurines, highly collectible, trade at high prices, and people travel to see collections of them.

The ceramic bust of Wilhelmina Geiszler, however, languishes in obscurity on a shelf in a glass case in Ashley's McIntosh County Heritage Center. This legendary artifact deserves to be showcased, for if it is tastefully publicized, travelers will come to Ashley to see it. The Heroine of the Prairies, the Martyr Mother of the Germans from Russia, as lovingly sculpted by the founder of Rosemeade Pottery, deserves a pedestal of her own.

⊱─━━◉━━─⊰

L ate in life, Mabel Bettenhausen Larson, then living in Cooperstown, wrote down her memories of growing up in a big German-Russian family in McIntosh County, North Dakota. She especially recalled how as a teenager she played hymns in the Beaver Creek Baptist Church.

"We had a [pump] organ at home where I taught myself to play," Mabel recalls. "The first song I could play with both hands was 'Jesus, Lover of My Soul.' My mother would let me know if it sounded right. She was in the kitchen cooking, baking, or doing something else. I loved to play that organ, and spent every spare moment practicing."

These are warm and vital memories, captured in verbal snapshots, but the difference between these and so many other prairie memoirs is that they happen to have been captured, also, by a documentary photographer of a government agency, the Farm Security Administration, in 1940. The photographer, John Vachon, took at least six wonderfully evocative photographs of Emma Grace Kramer Bettenhausen, the mother of Mabel. The negatives repose in the Library of Congress. There, as in Mabel's memoir, Emma Bettenhausen remains forever the German-Russian mother of timeless remembrance.

The photographers of the FSA have a checkered reputation, historically. In 1936, in the middle of the Great Depression, the FSA sent them out to take as many photographs of human misery as they could, thereby to bolster public support for the assistance programs offered by President Franklin Roosevelt's New Deal.

The negative public reaction to this propaganda program caused the FSA to redirect its photographers, such as Vachon, into a different line of work, seeking to document the continuing vitality of American life at the grassroots. Somehow, Vachon decided McIntosh County, North Dakota, was a good place to do this, and somehow, he was led to the Bettenhausen farmhouse southwest of Wishek.

So here we see Mrs. Bettenhausen laboring at her impressive cast-iron range; filling the stove with corncobs; ironing, with her flatirons heating atop the stove; inspecting, with evident pride, the canned goods, cabbages, and potato bin in her root cellar; checking a batch of bread dough in a big washpan. Here, too, we see a girl in a print dress, playing a grand pump organ, sitting on a thick book to reach the keyboard. To view the photographs, informed by that girl-woman's memoir, is simply transporting.

This, too, is splendid documentary photography, as illustrated by the two photographs of Mrs. Bettenhausen checking her dishpan of dough. She lifts the towel covering the dough, and it is a little tacky, sticking to the towel, but the look on her face says she is satisfied with it. That is because she is working with a *Vorteig*, a sticky batter-dough, to which, having completed the first rise, she now will add the rest of the flour for the second rise. That was the way it was done.

There are children in the photographs, lots of them, and on first examining the images, I thought that the Mrs. Bettenhausen depicted therein must have been the grandmother to some of them, but not so. She would have been about thirty-seven at the time, and she had borne sixteen children to her farmer-husband, Oliver Wesley Bettenhausen.

Emma Bettenhausen — Mrs. Bettenhausen, as she is known in the Library of Congress catalog — did not live to see any of her children to adulthood. She died in 1941 at age thirty-eight. Mabel, who had been working in Minneapolis, came home to care for the family. She does not bemoan her lot, any more than her mother would have.

⊱⊶⊷○⊶⊷⊰

The night of November 17, 1946, Jacob H. Lang, a German-Russian farmer south of Lehr, never went to bed. Instead he loaded some cattle and set off in his truck for West Fargo, intending to be first in line next morning at the packinghouse. At home in the Lang farmhouse, Jacob's wife Pauline and their nine children, ranging in age from thirteen years down to ten months, went to bed about ten o'clock.

Early next morning someone got a phone message through to Jacob that there was a fire at his house, so he started for home immediately, growing more uneasy about the welfare of his family as he drove.

Arriving home around 7:30 a.m., he found the one-story farmhouse burned to the ground, so he hastened to the home of his brother Gottlieb.

There he found three of the children all right, but inquired anxiously about the others. "These are all that are left," his brother replied — "whereupon," the *Ashley Tribune* reported, "Lang was visibly shaken and near collapse." Within a few days both Pauline and Jacob were admitted to hospital in Eureka, South Dakota, in a state of nervous collapse.

Then there was Chester, twelve years old, formerly the second-oldest child, now the oldest surviving, as his sister Orpha had perished. He was the only family member capable of talking about what happened.

He and two other children, seven-year-old Betty and the infant Robert, had been asleep on the ground floor of the house. The other children were sleeping in the basement. Around midnight Pauline discovered the house afire, with the fire blocking the door, whereupon Chester had the presence of mind to sweep up his baby brother and climb out a window. His mother and sister Betty followed. While they stood outside, the others perished in the fire.

They were Orpha Darlene, thirteen; Arbedella Arlene, ten; Darold Delbert, eight; Janice Ivela, six; Donna Mae, four; and Bernice, one year old.

A neighbor, Ben Koepplin, saw the fire and rushed over. He arrived too late to do anything but gather up the survivors and take them to shelter. The cause of the fire was uncertain, but likely had to do with the stove fire banked overnight.

More than sixty years later, Delmar Zimmerman pointed to the name of Orpha Lang on a memorial stone and said, "She was in my Sunday school class." Delmar told me the rudiments of the story of the Lang family tragedy and later sent me a clipping from the *Ashley Tribune*.

The Lang family plot is in the George Station German Baptist Cemetery, seven miles south of Lehr, at the end of a mile-long prairie trail. Its site is gorgeous, in the middle of a pasture and right alongside a blue kettle lake.

Until recently the cemetery was in a shambles and was practically inaccessible. Delmar led other descendants of German Baptist pioneers of the locality in a campaign to clean up the cemetery, fence and mark it, and get the county to reopen access.

The day we drove out to the George Station German Baptist Cemetery, killdeers decoyed us away from their nests, bobolinks trilled, and Delmar pointed with pride to the graves of his grandparents, Gottlieb and Katharena Zimmermann. They gave the acreage for the establishment of the cemetery.

Despite its beautiful situation and its well-kept condition, this burial ground will always be identified with tragedy. Here are the graves of Pauline and Jacob, and a single marker for the six children who died in the fire, along with two others who died in infancy. The family stone bears the legend, "I am the resurrection and the life."

I am going to stop now and think about these things for a while.

><>-O-<><

In passages immediately above, I have fallen into the narrative habits of the Germans from Russia, foregrounding hardship and tragedy. In constructing such mythic accounts, they certainly have plenty to work with — an endless supply of injustices and misfortunes strung across continents and oceans, all the way here to the Coteau, where graveyards are their most referenced cultural marks. I now remind myself, it is not all a tale of woe. Resilience, persistence, aspiration, and faith also figure in the story.

It was my privilege to participate in a research day at the Central Grasslands Research Extension Center, near Streeter, North Dakota. The Central Grasslands Center is a branch station devoted to, well, the central grasslands of North Dakota, which are pretty much defined by the region known as the Missouri Coteau. To lovers and shooters of waterfowl, two groups that overlap a great deal, this is the Prairie Pothole region, the breeding ground of the Central Flyway. To ranchers and other agriculturalists, the Coteau is a distinctive agricultural region, mixed crops and livestock with emphasis on beef cattle.

I brought out a couple of exhibit panels featuring historic photographs copied from county extension agent reports in the Coteau during the 1930s and 1940s. The first panel was entitled, "Hard Times in the Coteau."

A key part of this story is the advent of New Deal farm programs, designed to ease the effects of drought and depression on farmers. Farmers welcomed the checks, of course, but there was considerable unease about some of the ways the farm program intruded into farm life.

In the first place, there was the sheer paperwork involved. The agent of Logan County in 1935 actually took some pride in handling the volume of paper required to administer the farm program. He sent out 9,328 individual letters and 20,724 copies of circulars. He had a picture taken of himself among the mountain of mailbags required for one mailing.

The paperwork perhaps seemed worth the effort to the county agents, as it made them more popular than ever before. Nearly 100 percent of farmers signed up for government commodity programs. They liked those checks.

They did not always like some of the requirements attached to the checks, such as the operations of the Drought Cattle Purchase Program. This program had several purposes, the first of which was to lower livestock inventories so as to raise the price of cattle. In drought areas such as the northern plains, the government also sought to take cattle off the hands of farmers who had no feed for them.

The problem was many of the cattle were in poor shape, and there was no market for such meat. So after purchasing a lot of bony cattle, the government would condemn them, hire guys to shoot them, and bury the carcasses in bulldozed pits.

In 1934, the Kidder County agent reported, government agents purchased 20,230 head of cattle. Most of these were shipped out to provide meat for people on relief, but 2,075 were condemned and shot on the farm.

In those days county agents all carried cameras to take photos to illustrate their annual reports. The photos generally were supposed to illustrate good practices and rural progress. In Kidder County in 1934, though, the agent made a point of taking, and pasting into his report, photographs of men shooting cattle and of the carcasses strewn across the ground. Although generally producers were pleased with the program, the tone of the agent's report indicates clearly that he was disgusted. Those were hard times in the Coteau, and people had to do hard things.

Besides the ghastly business of liquidating cowherds in the 1930s under the Drought Cattle Purchase program, the photographs in my exhibit depicted such developments as poisoning grasshoppers with homemade tub broadcasters and making mattresses with surplus cotton shipped in from the southern states.

The other exhibit panel I brought out to Streeter was called "Keeping the Faith in the Coteau." Both the hard-times panel and the keeping-the-faith panel were compiled from the same source — the annual reports of county extension agents during the 1930s. Whereas the first panel told nothing but sad stories, the second one depicted how people kept their spirits up and kept the feeling of community alive even in the worst of times.

For instance, I get tickled every time I look at a photo of this darling girl from Kidder County, Arlene Rothi, overall-clad, showing her beef cattle at 4-H achievement days. She is the only girl in the photos. And she keeps winning top honors for her steers.

Then there are all those photos of women in homemaker clubs. These clubs had to have been important during the worst years of the depression. Club meetings were a reason to put on something better than a housedress, and while they brought together people enduring the worst depression in history, they focused on finer things.

Men, too, kept the faith individually and collectively. They participated in cooperative projects such as cattle-dipping, which required group investment. All those photographs of farmers operating homemade contraptions to combat grasshoppers are evidence, yes, that the infestation of insects was severe, but also that farmers had lost neither hope nor their powers of invention.

Over the past quarter-century or so there has been a change in how we think about the Great Depression of the 1930s. Until recently, when historians spoke of the Great Depression, the plotline was simple: the people of the United States were knocked prostrate by the depression, and lay senseless on the ground until Franklin Roosevelt's New Deal picked them up, dusted them off, and got them working again. Ordinary people were helpless to save themselves without the power of the government.

Then historians began to notice that despite the depression and even the Dust Bowl, ordinary people retained initiative and did a lot of things to hold their families and communities together. Not that they did not welcome help — personally I have never sent a check back to the US Department of Agriculture! — but they were not helpless, either.

That is what I see in these historic photographs from the Missouri Coteau — people doing things, people deserving of sympathy, not merely pity.

One day in 1937 Professor Alfred Arvold, founder of the Little Country Theater at North Dakota Agricultural College, drove out to the pavilion on the shores of Lake Hoskins, in McIntosh County. He was scheduled to speak there on the one-word subject, "Neighborhoods." When he arrived, there were four hundred people awaiting him. People keeping the faith in the Coteau.

>⊷⊶○⊷⊶<

In 1965 my mother agreed with the Missouri Synod Lutheran pastor who confirmed me that I was an excellent prospect for the ministry. That would have ended badly, I fear. Through my adult life I caused my mother considerable grief on account of my wayward progress and poor decisions. One afternoon late in her life, however, I saw a quizzical look cross her face as she remarked over iced tea, "I guess you really are sort of like a preacher, aren't you?"

Yes, I am attentive to the landmarks of faith that spangle the landscape, and to the voices of the faithful who inhabit it. I love a good parable. I am driven to bring edifying stories to the people, and not averse to chiding them now and then. I realize, especially in recent years, that I define my role as a historian of the Great Plains in pastoral terms as much as scholarly. If I confess that I am trying to do good history, there is more than one level of meaning in the statement. Professor Arvold, who brought his message of encouragement to the Coteau in 1937, as he did in hundreds of times and places, would understand just what I am talking about.

5. THE STAR ON THE BARN

Wherein the prairie historian finds the fibers of community
on the post-rural plains

A few years ago my Suzzanne and I were happy and honored to be artists in residence at the Wallace Stegner House in Eastend, Saskatchewan. We did some good writing that summer. Suzzanne took Wally's upstairs bedroom as her office, while I set up shop in Hilda's dining room.

Wallace Stegner, a Pulitzer Prize-winning author and the dean of Western letters, spent key years of his boyhood during the second decade of the twentieth century here in Eastend. We are great fans and close students of his memoir, if you can call it that, *Wolf Willow*, a work we have taken apart and put back together again countless times.

During this and other sojourns in Eastend, we have dined on many occasions in Jack's Cafe, a well-known establishment dating from the origins of the town, run by generations of Greek proprietors. Above the counter hangs a portrait of the Parthenon. I have no doubt that this Greek establishment contributed to the titling of *Wolf Willow*'s final chapter as "False Front Athens."

Stegner's most ardent admirers have a hard time with this chapter, wherein he considers the possibilities of life in a country town like Eastend and concludes it was a pretty good place to be a boy, but not a place where a thinking person could live a rewarding adult life. There is a lot of ambivalence in the chapter, but in the end, it comes off as patronizing at best.

Stegner assesses his old hometown in line with his general assumptions about life on the plains. He lived his boyhood on what he considered the last frontier, where the ideal of progress reigned. In retrospect, Stegner questioned all that and embraced what scholars like me have come to call the declensionist narrative. On the plains we have fashioned a legend of failure, come to think that our best days are behind us, and embraced the belief that our region is in a permanent state of decline.

The declensionist narrative poses all sorts of problems for plains folk who never have heard the scholarly phrase, but have lived the arc of its narrative. How do you maintain social capital, hold communities together, and live satisfying lives in a declensionist country?

⇒—⊷—○—⊷—⇐

Y ou drive through one of these little plains country towns today, with its businesses boarded up, its residential streets gap-toothed from people moving the houses away into the county seat, and you get no clue of the vitality that once surged through the place. So it is with Gascoyne, North Dakota. But if you talk to someone like Phyllis Teigen, who grew up there, the place comes alive with stories.

Gascoyne is on the Milwaukee Railroad, and when the rails arrived in 1907, Phyllis's father, Atwood LeRoy Cady, was already there, holding down a claim and running a store. He married Laura May Hankel in Aberdeen, South Dakota, in 1917, and moved her to a home in Gascoyne, where Phyllis was born.

Town life ran on railroad time. For instance, as a girl Phyllis was supposed to hang the mailbag for the Flyer, the 9:30 train coming out of the west. She had to stand on a box to reach the mail carrier alongside the tracks. A mechanical arm extended from the passing train to sweep the mailbag from the carrier where it had been tied. "It's a dangerous thing," Phyllis says, because of the suction of the passing train. After it passed, she would pick up the incoming Gascoyne mailbag the conductor had tossed out onto the ground.

One morning Phyllis went up to hang the mail and the depot agent told her it was not time yet. Suddenly the agent hollered, "Tie that mail! The train's coming!"

"I got it tied, and just jumped down, and there was the train," Phyllis recalls. When her father found out about that dangerous close call, she got a heck of a scolding.

The railroad connected the town to the outside world, which had both good and unfortunate aspects — such as the many tramps that descended from boxcars when trains stopped in the 1930s. The Cady house was one of the first that the bums would come to as they entered town, and Mrs. Cady always gave them something.

Sometimes, though, they unnerved her. Once the whistle was signaling the train's imminent departure, and this one bum would not leave the porch — he kept demanding a coat. Finally Mrs. Cady grabbed a coat from a hook by the door and threw it to him so he would leave. It was Phyllis's coat.

By this time the automobile was bringing to town another stream of humanity — gypsies, they were called then, now more respectfully called Romani. As elsewhere on the plains, local people viewed traveling gypsies — however incorrect that term and attitude may be today — as mysterious, shady, and a threat to property. "They were a different breed," Phyllis said, reflecting the language and values of her time.

In the 1930s Mr. Cady ran a garage, and after school he left teenage Phyllis in charge while he drove a mail route. This was good for the after-school trade. She sold a lot of candy and ice cream. Once she even managed to patch a tire. She had strict instructions, though, that if gypsies came, she was to lock the garage and the gas pump while somebody called the sheriff.

By the next decade Phyllis was married and her husband, Mervin Teigen, introduced a third means of mechanized transport—the airplane—for carrying the mail. One winter in the late 1940s it was so snowy Phyllis, who subbed a mail route for her father, could not get through. So Mervin took the mail up in his Cessna 140 fitted with skis.

Flying over the farms and ranches, he dropped mail, groceries, and, in at least one case, cigarettes. One farmer was a heavy smoker and was getting desperate for a smoke by the time Mervin dropped him a carton. A neighbor watched the guy run for the drop and later told Mervin, "I think he had that cigarette lit before it hit the ground!"

><----<>--0--<>---->

Such a little school, and it had two songs.

Mabel Hoth wrote the "Buffalo Springs Pep Song" to the tune of "Because There's Something About a Soldier."

> Oh! The team from Buffalo Springs
> Makes the ball go through the rings.

And Alice Joyce wrote the "Buffalo Springs High School Song" to the tune of "Home on the Range."

> And down by a pool we have founded a school
> And christened it Buffalo Springs.

You drive by the site of Buffalo Springs today—an old Milwaukee Railroad town, south side of present Highway 12, just up the road from Gascoyne in Bowman County, North Dakota—and there is little to excite curiosity. One building survives, a two-room former café that was composed of two homestead shacks joined together and stuccoed over. Look closer, and there's the town pump.

Standing on such ground, can you see, hear, or even just sense the life that once teemed there? I think I can. I think places like this, with only meager material remains, speak. I am not talking about ghosts in any conventional understanding of such, but rather the human sense of place, something one can cultivate by opening up to it. The apparently wide-open spaces of the Great Plains are covered, in fact layered, with articulate places.

Still, I am a historian, and I welcome the stories and documents that give flesh to the spirits of place. Charity Fries, of Scranton — daughter of the Buffalo Springs depot agent — has told me stories of the place, and now comes her letter atop a big red scrapbook in a big brown package.

The scrapbook was compiled by Melvin "Red" Ingebretson and Roba Ingebretson, who arrived from Wisconsin in 1933 to breathe life into the school by the pool (a little lake, the water supply for railroad engines). Red was superintendent and also taught math and science. Roba taught history, geography, and literature. During their tenure in the mid-1930s, the school expanded from two to three rooms and graduated its first high school class. You can tell the kids loved the Ingebretsons, because they wrote stories about them and made fun of them. One joke began with a second-grader playing school, and the mistress of her class remarking, "Well, Margery, I suppose you're the teacher." To which the lass replied, "I'm not smart enough to be teacher. I'm only the superintendent."

Red Ingebretson was the force behind an ambitious athletic program, at the heart of which was basketball for girls and boys. The Duchesses and the Dukes made the ball go through the rings, but not that consistently. While they did well against the Gascoynes and the Marmarths of their schedule, playing in the Southwest Conference organized by Ingebretson, larger schools like Hettinger or

Bowman dealt them some hard losses. You get the feeling, though, that when Red lectured the players it was character and improvement that mattered more than wins and losses; he believed it, and so did they.

It was in kittenball (softball) that Buffalo Springs excelled, with both a high school and a town team. Red got the local merchants to throw in for floodlights so night games could be played on the school grounds. Could the Dukes hit? The table of batting averages for 1935 shows two of them batted .750.

Plays, dances, debates, play days — look at these photos, these mimeo flyers, these posters that plastered depots up and down the line. No wonder I hear voices.

> There's something about the Dukes
> That is fine, fine, fine.

⊱──•◦•──⊰

"I t'll be a cold day in hell when I pay 15 cents for a cup of coffee." It may not be obvious to you why that sentence is hilarious. It is a matter of context — the context in this case being *Memories of the Hotel,* a remarkable venture in theatre and memory staged in Mott, North Dakota. What a happy privilege it was to be there for the opening of the show in the gymnasium of the buff-brick Mott-Regent High School.

"The Hotel" is the Holiday House, which stood on Mott's main street until early morning November 6, 1989, when it burned down. It was, to begin with, an impressive building for a small town — three stories high, hip roof, deep soffits, corner location, wide veranda wrapped around the second story, supported by heavy pillars. Called by various names — Brown Hotel, Wicks Hotel, and finally Holiday House — it anchored the business district and was the center of the community.

After the fire the local paper commented, "We will miss this grand old hotel, which was the focus of many a coffee break, meeting place for organizations and clubs and a place dependable for their delicious meals."

That summary did not begin to capture the significance of the old hotel—a fact that became plain as a local writers' club, which calls itself the Writer's Enclave, began writing stories about the place. Once released from memory, anecdotes about the hotel buzzed around like bees without a hive, until one member of the group, Joyce Hinrichs, proposed they be housed in a play. She provided a structure for the script; the writers filled in the vignettes based on recollections. Even as the composition entered production, it continued to evolve, as actors and participants inserted their own memories and flourishes. "Nobody can say, I wrote this play," says Joyce, "because everybody wrote this play."

Early in the production, the narrator introduced Frank and Lorraine Masad, proprietors of the Holiday House from 1958 to its demise. They beamed; the audience stood and cheered. It was clear at the outset that the community regarded them as symbols of the identity and joy that had resided in the hotel. Frank joked that if he could have foreseen this, he would have been nicer to people when he was running the hotel.

Embedded in the play was a lot of inside humor. Several times an outsider in the crowd—and it was a crowd, filling the gym—would have wondered what the heck was so funny. This is a sign that the play was doing exactly what it was supposed to do. This was not a show staged for tourists. It was a conversation among the community. Code-talk, insider humor, these things assert identity, they say we are a peculiar people, we are who we are.

Names are important to such an enterprise. A big paper banner covered one wall and bore the names of all known employees of the hotel. Nearly all were German-Russian or German-Hungarian. Frank Masad is of Syrian ancestry. In the play, as he and Lorraine arrive to take over the hotel, one of the cardplayers in the lobby says, "You're not German then, are you?"

Before the play I chatted with Lanny Johnson, stage manager, grocer. He described the hotel as the "heart and soul" of Mott. I asked him, when the hotel burned down, where did that soul, all those transactions and affections that constitute a community, where did they go? Some of them found other homes, he said, but some of them "just disappeared into the air." This play, *Memories of the Hotel*, gave those things a home again. What happened here goes beyond art, beyond sentiment. It is a matter of spirit.

⊱—⋅⊙⋅—⊰

Here I realize why the final chapter of Wallace Stegner's *Wolf Willow*, "False Front Athens," is a painful disappointment. Stegner returned, in middle age, to the place of his boyhood on a quest of personal identity. This is a life-development thing, the uneasy middle-aged contemplation of identity. He emerged to say, "I may not know who I am, but I know where I am from." Good enough, we may say.

Prowling the paths of his youth, however, the middle-aged Stegner did not fully engage. He tried to remain incognito, to sleuth around town in search of informants and documentation, without reentering the community. Unlike the amateur (remember the Latin root of that word) authors of Mott, the acclaimed author from Eastend remained aloof from the memory community. Memory is the basis for community in prairie towns. Conversely, it takes a community to sustain memory as anything meaningful beyond the personal, trivial, or antiquarian.

><-+-◄>-◦-◄<+-◄

On May 24, 2007, when United States Senator Kent Conrad rose to recognize the community of Pisek on the occasion of its centennial, there were certain bases he had to tag. He touched on St. John Nepomucene Catholic Church, although he neglected to mention the Alphonse Mucha painting in the sanctuary. He made reference to Pisek's famous roast pork and potato dumpling suppers. And of course, the J-Mart, the Christmas candy capital of North Dakota. "The local J-Mart draws customers throughout the area," noted the senator, "because it is known for having the best Christmas candy selection in the region."

All right, there's the official notice, but it is a bit bland. Buying Christmas candy in Pisek is a pilgrimage for thousands of northern plains folk. They come not just for candy, but more so to plug into a living tradition, to feel part of history. They want to gaze up at the landscape mural painted on the west wall by Aileen Jelinek, hear the wood floors creak, and mill around with happy people. The Christmas candy trade at the red-brick J-Mart Store peaks early, in November; Veterans Day and Thanksgiving weekends are "really big," say the proprietors, Teresa Brandt and Bonnie Jelinek, with hundreds of customers crowding in.

Notice, too, the other ways in which the establishment carries tradition for the local citizens of this Moravian and Bohemian community founded in the 1880s. On the shelves are pouches of sugared fruit ready to be pressed into kolaches, and great cans of poppyseed for the use of local women, who make kolaches of the closed-face variety. The freezer is stocked with Leo's Potato Dumplings and Leo's Czech Fries from just over in Lankin. Pickled herring and headcheese, too, are big sellers.

The members of the Jelinek clan who operate this wonderful establishment are fully aware of their vital role in tradition. To illus-

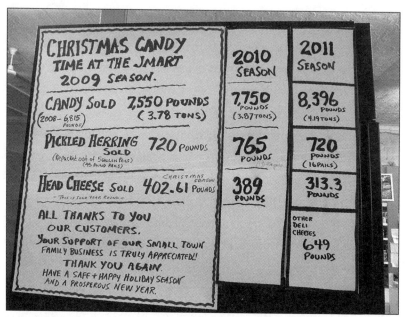

Holiday sales board (Christmas candy and ethnic specialties) at J-Mart of Pisek

trate, here is the handwritten historical sketch they have posted in the store.

> Al & Aileen Jelinek bought the J-Mart grocery store in 1946. They called it Pisek General Store, then Pisek Shopping Center & later J-Mart, Inc., in 1980. Al started the candy tradition in 1947. He bought 1200 lbs. of bulk choc. crème drops & hard candy because treats like this were scarce after WW II. More varieties of candy were added year after year. We have 67 kinds (chocolates, hard candy, & jellys) — over 3½ tones (7300 lbs.) of candy. We also have 9 kinds of bulk nuts. We also sell over 850 lbs. of bulk pickled herring. We sell bulk cheeses & headcheese also. Our candy season starts at the beginning of November & usually gone by second week of December even though more candy is added

every year. People come from all over — Devils Lake, Walhalla, G. Forks, Cavalier & stop in for their yearly trip of candy.

Al, who passed away in 2005, and Aileen, who lived on in the back of the store, raised thirteen children who have all worked in the establishment. The family-owned J-Mart grocery store is run by Teresa Brandt, a daughter, and Bonnie Jelinek, a daughter-in-law. Bonnie's husband, Francis, owns and operates the grocery store and the J-Mart carpet store, across the street, with his brother, Dominic Jelinek, who also is an installer for the carpet store.

Before we leave, Francis takes me up to the modest apartment, a former stock room, where Al and Aileen raised their thirteen children. Aileen, too, now has passed away, and the apartment remains exactly as she left it.

⊱──◆──○──◈──⊰

When I drove over to Canaan Moravian Brethren Church for the Christmas Eve Service, I expected to encounter one sublime event, for I had heard of the candlelight carol ritual so dear to Moravian hearts. I got more than I bargained for: two sublime events, one of them entirely unexpected, and not only by me.

Arriving early at the gorgeous red-brick church, stained light spilling onto the snowy ground, I went in and asked Pastor Chuck Belzer who could tell me about the candles, and was directed to a fine old gentleman, Virgil Hans. He explained that the candles used for Christmas Eve were beeswax, "because they're pure"; that the red frill wrapped around them not only catches the dripping wax but also "stands for the blood of Christ"; and that during the climactic hymn, "Morning Star," all would lift their candles over their heads. "Everyone lets their light shine," he mused.

A lovely service, it was. Knowing how the parishioners at Canaan love to torment their preacher, I am tempted to say that one thing making the service lovely was Pastor Chuck having such a terrible cold he lost his voice and could not preach. Well, I will say that, not because I do not like to hear Pastor Chuck preach, but because we got something else, that other thing I spoke of before, instead.

A succession of laypeople delivered the readings, and we sang carols between, and there was an offering for a family who had suffered some medical misfortunes. I wished the service could go on and on, but let me get right to the sublime thing I came for. A mixed choir came to the front and faced us. As the choir sang "The Birthday of a King" and then "A Thousand Candles," several young women distributed the beeswax candles to all in the pews. Next they came to the front, where each lit a candle from one held by Pastor Chuck, after which she moved through the congregation again, sharing the light.

As the house lamps were extinguished, and candlelight danced from every cheek and played upon the pale plaster walls, a men's choir of four remained at front. The congregation began to sing "Morning Star, O cheering sight! Ere Thou cam'st how dark earth's night!" and then repeated those lines. Then the four men sang scalewise, "Jesus mine," and the congregation sang, "In me shine," then the men, "In me shine," then the people, "Jesus mine, Fill my heart with light divine." There were three more stanzas, during the last of which all held their candles above their heads. People were crying, and I was one of them.

I was set up by what had come before, when Pastor Chuck was unable to preach. A daughter of the congregation, Janessa Gohdes, had offered to make some remarks in lieu of a sermon. Now, I think it would be fair to say that during her teenage years, in the heart of Ms. Gohdes, the spark of youthful rebellion occasionally had flared. Indeed, as I watched her stride assertively up the church aisle, miniskirted and booted, her hair maroon-streaked, I did not see that she was making any concessions of style to a conservative Moravian parish. Wait now, listen to her remarks.

Male quartet at Canaan Moravian Brethren Church: "Fill my heart with light divine"

Like a veteran pastor, she invokes the season, traditions of the parish, talks of Christmas pageants of the past where uncles embarrassed themselves, names older parishioners with joshing affection. She cajoles us to be better to and for one another — "How many of you and your family bake together?" she asks. And then she launches a litany of Christmas Eve recollections, from which I give but a sample.

- sitting on the ice cream maker while someone churns it
- playing with the baby Jesus from the manger scene and getting into trouble for it
- pug dogs in little outfits
- Grandma complaining that she has too many gifts

- church service at Canaan
- the star on the barn that we always tried to find on the way home

Janessa, I believe you have found it.

━━◆━○━◆━━

S uch a pleasure to return to Canaan Moravian Brethren Church a year later, this time on a sunlit First of Advent, the church buzzing with activity. We came to launch my new CD set produced by Prairie Public, *Candles at Canaan: Signs of Life in a Lonesome Land.* As so often happens on the prairies, we came for one thing and walked into all sorts of other delights.

The title audio essay of *Candles at Canaan*, the one printed above, dwells upon the beauty of the candlelight carol sung to conclude the Christmas Eve service. As we descend into the church basement this morning, on one side the children are happily at work crafting Christmas ornaments, and on the other an equally jolly crew of adults is assembling the candles for Christmas Eve.

Three hundred candles, ordered every year from a supplier in Wisconsin, have to be fitted with frills of red crepe paper, for reasons both symbolic and practical. The workers explain that as the beeswax symbolizes the purity of Christ, and the flame the eternal light of Christ, the red trim symbolizes the sacrifice of his blood.

At a table by himself sits John Saewert, entrusted with a sharp object. He unfolds the red crepe paper, cuts it into patches, folds them, and scores the edges with a paper cutter, so that when unfolded, they burst into curly frills.

The paper pieces are then passed to a table where they are applied to the candles. Introductions reveal the identities of the crew: Diane Strehlo, Kim Haugland, Sadie Gohdes, Sharon Saewert, Barb Larson, John Saewert, Paul Schroeder, Chuck Albright, and finally, we are told, "This is Dave Larson, all he does is walk around."

There is a deft ritual to fitting the candles. A cut patch of crepe paper is unfolded, placed flat on the table, and a candle rolled across to flatten it. The patch next is folded back the opposite way from what it was. Then it is wrapped around the base of a candle and taped into place, the frilly side upward.

The fitted candle is placed into a square wooden board into which, in a farm shop, twenty-five holes have been bored and green paint applied. The workers fill eight boards and then put the balance of the candles into bowls. This is enough for everyone who attends on Christmas Eve and also all the parishioners Pastor Chuck Belzer may visit at home or in care homes.

So the carol ritual is not just a moment in one evening. It is something that stretches across time, giving people roles in the community and reminders of what is important. This is the way with so many community rituals. There is a public aspect to them, where many partake in the food, the activity, or in this case, the light. And behind the scenes there is a whole other side, mostly invisible to the world, whereby members of a group engage in communion. It is a specific joy to stumble into these proceedings, but it is a matter of general satisfaction to know that across the prairies, this sort of thing goes on all the time, whether we know it or not.

Over in the corner of the kitchen, parishioners, mostly women, are preparing for the potluck that will follow the First of Advent service. I asked if there are any signature dishes that are sure to appear on the buffet table, and several preparers chime in to answer, "Deer sausage." 'Tis the season.

The service is sweet, the potluck sumptuous, and Advent, the joy of early winter, is commenced.

⊳⊢⋄⊷○⊷⋄⊣⊲

December 24, 2005, Gavin Johnson was on duty in southern Iraq. An air national guardsman on his second tour in-country as a member of a security unit, he was thankful to be relieved from his post for a little while in order to make a phone call. Back at quarters he shed helmet and body armor and placed the call to his grandpa, Kenny Johnson, in Walsh County, North Dakota.

Grandpa Johnson was waiting outside North Trinity Lutheran Church, also known as the Swede Church, for Gavin's call. He held his cell phone up, and over there in Iraq, Gavin heard the bells of North Trinity pealing a Christmas greeting. Grandpa was on duty, too, and God was in his heaven, after all.

Gavin told me all this on Christmas Eve of 2006, sitting in the sanctuary of North Trinity, while once again the bells rang out. As I write of it, I am seized repeatedly by feelings of inadequacy, not just the usual ones that come with being Lutheran, but specific ones having to do with my inability to capture for you what went on there. I have sound recordings, high-resolution photographs, video files, notes, and sketches, but all this data does not sum up to what happened.

Colors, for instance. The landscape was bleak on a gray afternoon, snow cover half-melted, but with dusk came forgiveness in shades of peach and aquamarine. Inside the church foyer, blue flame from a propane torch and yellow light from a bare bulb made the white tongue-and-groove walls creamy. The outside porch light illuminated the colorful parkas of folks standing between the church and the cemetery like they were ghosts outfitted by Eddie Bauer. Flushed by chill, warmth, and emotion, even pale Swedish cheeks became prairie roses.

Sounds, of course. The bells pealing for forty minutes or more, trucks and cars coming and going, feet tramping in and out, exclamations of recognition, a few sobs. In cars parked around, and among people standing around, multiple conversations of which only half is heard, as cellphone callers work through lists of family members and former neighbors, reestablishing ties with kin and friends. (Some of those dialed answer to hear the bells and talk a bit, while others refrain from picking up, so that the bells of North Trinity will be captured in their voicemail and they can play them for family gatherings on Christmas Day.)

And then the stories. Sitting in the sanctuary with Kenny Johnson, Marjorie Kulberg, and Shelley McCann, we heard how the calling custom began. "There was a lady who was living behind the church here in the early years," Kenny recounts. "She would stand outside and listen to the bell." In 1972 this woman, Nellie Almen, was living in California, and Kenny had a new mobile phone in his pickup. As the bell tolled that Christmas Eve, Kenny rang her up to hear it. "From there on," he says, "it mushroomed."

Nowadays the church, which officially closed in 1953, is busy only at Christmas Eve, Memorial Day, and one Sunday in June for a reunion service. The June service echoes an annual celebration Kenny remembers from back in the 1940s. There would be a worship service, a meal, and then a day spent picnicking on the grounds. There would be homemade ice cream, and a banana bunch would be hung in a tree.

"I come out here good times and sad times," says Shelley. "It's been a comfort to me for years."

"My parents were buried here, I'll be buried here," chimes in Marjorie. "It's important to have this history."

May I say, long may it ring. Here in Walsh County, in Iraq, in Connecticut, in Pennsylvania, in Oregon, in California. This is North Trinity calling.

⊱⊶⊷◦⊷⊶⊰

B eneath the spreading branches of boxelders, gentle talk hung in the air like perfume. The peonies in the nearby cemetery were budding, not yet in bloom. Some people nursed the remnants on their plates from the potluck, while others strolled among the gravestones, conversing with departed relatives. Now and then someone looked up at the steeple, carefully restored atop the white-frame church, although there have been no regular services in the church for more than half a century.

One Sunday every June, the memory group of North Trinity Lutheran Church, in Walsh County, southwest of Nash, gathers for a service of remembrance and a potluck reunion. The activities on this day are familiar ones for our part of the country — people renew the ties of a once vital, now reminiscent community, and they share a meal. This is, however, an unusual memory group.

These are the people with whom we visited on Christmas Eve 2006 in order to partake of a wonderful tradition. Young Gavin Johnson that evening told us how the previous year, when he was on duty in Iraq, he rejoiced to hear the bells of home courtesy of the cellphone of his grandfather, Kenny Johnson.

Thanks to Shelley McCann, who invited us out for the picnic this year. The only unwelcome guests here are the gnats of June. What a contrast in the landscape from that of December! The cemetery is kept neat, but all around it the growth is lush. Back of the church the Middle Park River runs high but well within its banks.

The service is joyous but subdued, because these folk are mostly Swedes, after all. Hymns are traditional — "Holy, Holy, Holy," "Beautiful Savior," and "Sweet Hour of Prayer." The service closes with table grace, after which the people, instead of exiting the way they came in, file into the old kitchen behind the altar, where the potluck buffet is arranged. Shelley has brought doughnuts, which we gather are some sort of tradition she is obliged to carry on forever, like the open-faced chipped beef sandwiches another lady has brought. Exiting from the back of the church, the people take places to eat in the grove of boxelders and crabs on the south side of the building.

Kenny and the other old-timers recall the picnic used to be closer to the river, in a cow pasture. They tell the favorite story of how every year someone bought a bunch of bananas and hung it in a tree. For a nickel, a kid was allowed to reach up and cut one. I love the idea of a bunch of bananas hanging from a boxelder in North Dakota.

The people of North Trinity received a small grant from an organization called Preservation North Dakota to restore their steeple in 2006. They raised most of the money themselves, though. As for the care and maintenance of the memory community, well, they are handling that quite nicely themselves, thank you.

⊱─◈─○─◈─⊰

In 1936 fifty high school coaches, administrators, and athletes gathered at the beautiful high school in Sykeston, North Dakota, for a clinic in six-man football. Before end of day the athletic director of Jamestown College had issued an invitation to hold the state six-man championship game on the college field. That fall Sykeston claimed the title by defeating Ray 39 to 19. Six-man football, the game of the plains, had arrived in North Dakota.

In the 1930s most high schools played only one sport, basketball. The girls' side of the game was in decline and would largely die out for more than a generation. On the other hand, there was increasing interest in boys' athletics, especially in football. This interest was fueled by the enthusiasm for big-time college football that had swelled since the advent of radio.

On the plains, though, football ran up against the regional problems of sparse population and long distances. Small high schools were unable to muster respectable rosters for a rigorous game requiring eleven players. Moreover, in the middle of the Great Depression, equipment costs for such large teams were daunting.

It was Stephen E. Epler, a high school administrator in Beatrice, Nebraska, who hit on the idea of adapting football to the plains by eliminating the guards and tackles and one back — six-man football, with every man but the center (and later the center, too) eligible. Field size was reduced to 40 by 80 yards, and it was required that the ball could not cross the line of scrimmage until the offense had executed a "clear pass" of three yards, that is, a lateral or a forward pass.

The result was a wide-open, high-scoring game with a lot of 140-pound hometown heroes. The first six-man game was played in Hebron, Nebraska, on September 16, 1934. That same fall some schools in Barnes County, North Dakota, played some exhibition games. The first league play was by schools along the Kansas-Nebraska border in 1935. After that, leagues organized rapidly from Texas to North Dakota.

Six-man football was fun, and people loved it, but its days were numbered. High school consolidation created somewhat larger schools that, even if they could not go eleven-man, were likely to turn to nine-man ball on the northern plains, eight-man on the southern plains. Six-man largely died out in the 1950s and 1960s, although it persists in several distinct precincts of the plains — most notably West Texas.

One of my students, Nathan Sand, looked into the history of six-man football in North Dakota and found it was played widely and enthusiastically. Among the schools that played the game were West Fargo, Donnybrook, Haynes, Deering, Sentinel Butte, Van Hook, Starkweather, Elbowoods, Dazey, Nome, Sykeston, Tuttle, Esmond, Grace City, Kensal, Hurdsfield, Cathay, Hannaford, Heaton, Ray, Grenora, Alamo, Alexander, Wildrose, Drake, Fort Yates, Maddock, Minnewauken, Kindred, Pembina, Rolette, Monango, Milnor, Max, and Velva.

Sand turned up many great details of the story. He learned, for instance, that by 1939, when Starkweather beat Pembina for the state title in the University of North Dakota stadium, the championship game drew 3,500 spectators. The following year, however, Drake and Kindred were declared co-champs because a blizzard foreclosed the scheduled title game in Jamestown.

Old guys who played the six-man game recall it with great fondness, and the heroic memories get better every year. Fortunately, details can generally be verified, or not, in the old newspapers.

When I first wrote about six-man football on the plains, the response showed this is a chapter of Great Plains life that still stirs senses and recollections. I got letters and messages from veterans of the game in North Dakota and across the plains.

For instance, R. Wallace "Pop" Gotham, now living in Chetek, Wisconsin, was the coach for all sports at Ray High School from 1935 to 1939, and he recalls the historic first, 1936, state six-man football title game.

The principal from Sykeston called him in early November and proposed they play an unofficial championship game. "We had 3-4 inches of snow at Ray but was told that Sykeston had none, so the logical thing was to play there," Gotham recounts. After a two-hundred-mile drive on bad highways in packed cars, the undefeated Ray team arrived to find folks at Sykeston using a road grader to scrape snow from the field. Gotham realized he had been snookered for the home field advantage.

The troubles for Ray had just begun. Besides some homer calls by the referees, there also was the rangy quarterback of Sykeston to deal with, a fellow tall enough to pass over the Ray players. The Ray quarterback, David Lemire, still lives there, and says he just got too cold and weary to keep chasing the guy from Sykeston.

"I always felt that I had let the team down by not demanding that we play on a neutral field," Gotham writes. "I thought that 6-man was a good game for the small schools so that a coach had enough players to practice without using players that were not in the best physical condition."

Speaking of questionable calls—I also heard from Elden Stompro, in Swan Lake, Montana, about the 1952 game matching Columbus and Bowbells. Stompro played for Coach Vern Hedstrom at Columbus High School, graduating in 1953. "Our big rival was Bowbells," he says. "Our game in Columbus in the fall of 1952 against Bowbells presented a problem that probably never happened before."

The field was rude: it had no goalposts or scoreboard. The arrangements, too, were makeshift: "Vern Hedstrom had forgotten to ask someone to be the official scorekeeper."

"It was, as usual, a wild high-scoring game," Stompro recounts, warming to the tale. "We got to the end of the game and no one knew for sure what the score was. The referee lined all of the players up and asked each one how many points they had scored.

"The first liar didn't have a chance! To this day no one knows who won that game."

Furthermore, Stompro writes, "I remember playing in a game in Donnybrook where there was a pump on the playing field."

Lest we think that six-man football was some sort of quaint frontier amusement with no lasting pertinence, I will point out that scores of schools still play it in West Texas, and a few in other states. Six-man football is still a going, and enthusiastic, enterprise.

So, I continue to inquire after these six-man stories, in search of answers to questions such as,

- Who was the guy who clipped Lowell Fruhwirth and broke his leg in the 1958 Sykeston-Bowden game?
- Just what was the mysterious butt-to-butt formation deployed by the boys from St. Francis Academy of Hankinson? I really want to know.

⊱┈⬦┈◦┈⬦┈⊰

Stories of six-man football on the northern plains just keep coming, affirming this was a chapter in regional history full of meaning to participants, who sense they were part of something distinctive.

A key booster of the game in North Dakota and nationwide was A.W. Larson, school superintendent at Sykeston. For the *Athletic Journal* he wrote that six-man "provides on a smaller scale all the thrills, fun, and excitement of the game."

American Boy magazine, published in Detroit, took a keen interest in the game, naming All-American teams in the early years, a form of recognition in which Dakotans, pioneers of the six-man game, fared particularly well. In 1937, for instance, *American Boy* named Richard Beck, a halfback from Haynes, North Dakota, to its All-American squad. In 1938 Eugene Rothstein, a quarterback from Haynes, was so honored. The magazine also named the 1939 Starkweather team one of the top ten in the nation.

Many local players and fans, once introduced to the six-man game, preferred it to the standard eleven-man. Commenting on this trend in North Dakota, *American Boy* explained, "In the older game the center, guards and tackles carry much of the drudgery of the game while the ends and backs make the scores and get the cheers and headlines. In six-man . . . everybody carries the ball! Everybody scores! The glory and the fun are passed around."

Sometimes even reluctant participants got in on the action. My student historian Nathan Sand recounts a story told to him by Duane Voigt about the 1951 state title game, Elbowoods versus New Salem. Elbowoods put the student manager into the game, even though he was terrified of being hit. He lined up where he thought he would be away from the action, but a pass bounced off another player's shoulder pad and into his hands. The startled boy then ran for a touchdown and kept right on going — off the field and out of the facility. Someone finally stopped him and brought him back because he had the only available game ball.

Leo Reinhold, who played for Hebron, told about the 1950 title game with Elgin. In the second quarter Hebron already was ahead by fifty-one points. The team from Elgin quit and went home. This was not an uncommon development in those days of high-scoring contests.

Six-man appealed to community boosters because it brought people to town. "The playing of six-man has a tendency to hold people in our community rather than for them to go elsewhere for their entertainment and shopping," wrote Larson in 1938. "Local business, especially, is enthusiastic about the game. Our games are important events in community life."

In the long run football could not save a town, but six-man was great while it lasted, and its partisans recall it with something more than nostalgia. Six-man football does not loom so large in regional myth as homesteading or the Dust Bowl, of course, but those who knew it claim for it a place in the regional story as a fair representation of prairie life — wide-open, full of opportunity, inventive, fun-loving. There is something in this experience that people know, even if they cannot quite articulate it, defines them as plains folk.

⊱─◈─◯─◈─⊰

Aspiration and adaptation brought six-man football into being on the Great Plains. Demographic and social change wrought its decline and disappearance from most parts of the region. High school sport, as the linchpin of social capital in many prairie communities, is symbolic of the maintenance issues faced by community builders. The state of nature is not stability; the state of nature, and community, is transition.

It remains common for commentators to refer to life in places like North Dakota as "rural." The term is no longer applicable. I remember rural life — card parties at the school, extension meetings in the home, party lines, all that stuff — but with farm consolidation, as well as declining birth rates, the demographic base for rural life on the plains is long gone. Nor is the situation quite "urban," either; the term just lacks face validity for life here. For lack of a better term, I refer to the society of the twenty-first-century Great Plains as "post-rural."

The nexus of community in matters material collapses into the hierarchy of towns and small cities remaining in the region. The community of memory, however, still pulses through the landscape and stirs souls. In this respect, William Faulkner's maxim about the American South holds also for the northern plains: "The past is not dead. It's not even past."

———————

One afternoon I heard Mike Robinson (archivist of North Dakota State University), Ann Braaten (curator of the Emily P. Reynolds Historic Costume Collection), and Tricia Velure (then a history graduate student) give a wonderful talk about the Alba Bales House. This was the practice house for home economics students at North Dakota Agricultural College. The home ec girls were required to spend time in residence at Alba Bales House to demonstrate they could be competent homemakers. Judging by what alums say, this group living was sort of a bonding experience.

They had a fair amount of fun, too, and one particular episode from 1949 caught my attention — a mock wedding. The mock wedding, you see, is a fine old folk custom characteristic of the northern plains states and the prairie provinces. Michael Taft of Saskatoon is the folklorist who has done the fieldwork on mock weddings in the region and published the results in *North Dakota History*.

A mock wedding is a parody, a bit of folk theater in which people dress up in ridiculous fashion and go through a ridiculous ceremony, generally as part of a wedding anniversary observance. Often, according to Taft, the mock wedding comes as an interruption of a banquet toast-and-roast of the anniversary couple.

Costume is a big element in the farce. Men don dresses to play the female parts, including the bride, and women put on trousers to play the male parts, including the preacher. The clergyman reads from a telephone book or a girly magazine. The father of the bride often carries a shotgun.

Another important element in a mock wedding is the vows. Taft says, "The mock wedding is one way in which women of the community can express their ambivalent and conflicting roles as farm wives. . . . Women are in charge of the mock wedding in most communities; one question that interests these women is 'What does it mean to marry a farmer and become a farm wife?'"

The vows, then, speak for the women. Generally they are written especially for the occasion, or as least customized to fit the couple being parodied. Frances Wold of Bismarck wrote one set of vows in which the bride promised the groom to "black his eyes and bloody his nose and pull his hair and stamp on his toes . . . and drink his beer and spend his dough and make his life a tale of woe." The groom, on the other hand, was to "wash the dishes and make the bed . . . and wish to heck that you were dead."

It is important that the author make the vows fit the people, place, and occasion — that is, localize them — and not just lift pre-pared lines. "To localize the script," Taft writes, "is to make it mean-ingful within the context of plains and prairie agrarian society."

Back to Alba Bales House — the occasion marked by the mock wedding in 1949 was the birthday of one of the resident girls. She re-called, "Jeanne wrote the ceremony in verse using Faye's and fiancé Bob's names as principal characters.

"The groom, 5'2" Meta Lou," said the birthday girl, "wore tan corduroy trousers with brown tweed jacket, plaid skirt, tan derby, and a boutonniere of red poppies. The victorious bride, Jeanne, chose a simple white broadcloth gown, fully cut, and a veil of lovely used curtain material cut with a clever jagged train. She carried a bouquet of orange carrots and pale green celery."

Obviously, these girls were proving themselves not only com-petent homemakers but also good community builders, capable of managing a regional ritual in good style.

Just how common were these mock weddings on the northern plains?

> At the September meeting, we held a "mock wedding" which has become a German-Russian custom, especially in North Dakota at 25th Anniversary parties. Everyone who attended had a great time and some good clean fun teasing each other about our "reversed roles" in the wedding.

This notice appeared in a 2003 newsletter of the Inland Northwest Chapter of the Germans from Russia Heritage Society, which meets in Spokane, Washington, and includes many folks with North Dakota roots. It indicates the continuing currency of the custom of mock weddings, in which gender roles are reversed, costumes and dialog concocted, in friendly satire of the institution of marriage.

The mock wedding is, of course, a German-Russian custom. Also a Norwegian custom, a German custom, and an Anglo-American custom. It is a regional phenomenon. Now, here is an account of a mock wedding in Mooreton, North Dakota, in 1928, as recorded in a published history of Richland County.

In August 1928 two young people from Mooreton, Lloyd McDougall and Genevieve Early, were married in Minneapolis. The groom was of Yankee stock, a Congregationalist family. The bride was a Catholic girl who had earned a teaching degree from the University of North Dakota and was teaching over in Minnesota. For those days, it was a distinctly mixed marriage.

About a week after the wedding the couple had a wedding dance for their friends back in Mooreton. To their surprise, the affair was rudely but happily interrupted by a mock wedding. While the band for the dance, the Johnny Starius Orchestra, played "Here Comes the Bride," a bogus minister, played by a chap named Hans Borgen, commenced the ceremony.

Most of the parts, male and female, were played by women. Carolyn Henkenius and Ella Bagg impersonated the parents of the groom. A flower girl, Rema Lenzen, strewed the floor with buckwheat. Helen Kloeppel played the bride, and Mabel Hoffman played the groom. Agnes Breuer bore the ring, and Amelia Henkenius carried flowers, daisies. Bridesmaids were Merle Evensen and Elizabeth Henkenius, each carrying wild sunflowers, and there were two best men, Rose Kloeppel and Margaret Kloeppel.

After the mock ceremony, participants went over to a business known as the Magnet, owned by the Lenzen family, and changed into more proper attire to dance the night away.

I mention all these names for a couple of reasons. First, there were various extended-family ties among the participants in the mock wedding. Second, the cast of the caper was a mixed lot, ethnically speaking. Research on the surnames reveals Austrians, Norwegians, and Anglo-Americans, reflecting the ethnic mix of the community. The mock wedding was a folk institution that bridged ethnic divisions — and provided no end of fun and hilarity for participants.

><+•>-O-<+•><

Senator Elroy Lindaas always said come over to one of his barn dances and I finally did. These gatherings take place eight or ten evenings a year during the months of June through September in the gambrel-roofed barn loft on Elroy's farm east of Mayville, North Dakota.

On this particular starry September night I ascended the barn stairs onto a polished plywood floor in the loft. There was Elroy fronting a band comprising different players at different times, including two accordions, base, fiddle, banjo, rhythm guitar, and mouth harp. I watched and listened and tried to think who Elroy reminded me of, and then it came to me: Ernest Tubb, whom years ago I observed at work in ET's Record Shop, Nashville. Not so much the voice, although Elroy has a fine baritone, mellow and just a little reedy; it is his carriage, the way he fronts and packs guitar, that reminds me of old ET.

Elroy Lindaas fronting the band at the Lindaas Barn Dance, Traill County, North Dakota

All around the perimeter of the loft is a grand mix of chairs—easy chairs, folding chairs, couches, rockers, love seats (more on the subject of romance later). You need good chairs to rest in, because folks here dance pretty hard.

The music comes in sets, mainly polkas, waltzes, two-steps. The polkas are mostly traditional, the waltzes both traditional and country, and the two-steps pure country and western. "Candy Kisses," for instance, or "Mansion on the Hill."

When the dancers start to flag, novelty numbers get them going again. "I think it's about time to do the butterfly," Elroy intones, and all the chairs empty. "Circle right!" he commands, "Now circle to your other right," he countermands, and people fall for it every time.

Guest artists come to the microphone to contribute sets, like a hulking trucker from western Minnesota who offered a set of country standards like "Green, Green Grass of Home," the next best thing to Porter Wagoner himself, and closed with "God Must Be a Cowboy at Heart" and dedicated it to his MOM, for Pete's sake. This sort of thing makes me glad I write nonfiction (mostly), because if I put something like that into a piece of fiction, some snippy critic would say it could not happen.

Oh, and those dancers. They are almost all social-security-eligible; some of them have been since the Nixon administration. This is eastern North Dakota, of course, and so there are no hats or caps in evidence, but plenty of enthusiasm. If I met these people outside I would lay money some of them could not climb the stairs to the loft, let alone dance the night away up there, but they do.

Some of them, too, put those love seats to good use. "We've had two romances spring up this summer," Elroy says, and past romances engendered in the loft have led to marriage. Late in the evening I noticed more middle-aged people showing up to collect their elders. I am not sure if it is because they did not want them driving that late, or because they wanted to keep tabs on their love lives.

Elroy was born and raised on this farm, which his grandfather homesteaded in 1878. The first barn dances originated with Elroy's daughters when they were in high school. Elroy had a musical history, however, having played in a three-piece band in high school days with his ag teacher and another student. "Then I got busy farming and laid such things aside," he recalls. Middle age does funny things, though; Elroy bought a banjo at a sale, and pretty soon the grownups were taking over the loft with their own music.

He is regionally famous or notorious or something for his song parodies, generally composed for some special event. This started when he got elected to the state senate. For the victory celebration, he says, "I put together a little song to the tune of 'The Wabash Cannonball,' and it was a hit." It is always a mistake to encourage that sort of thing, because now Elroy has a repertoire of about twenty such numbers, many of them anthems for the minority party in the state, which generally does have better music than the majority party anyway.

It is so dark and still here in the farm lot, but the loft light spills buttery onto the ground, and its beams release laughter across the beet and bean fields.

>―+‹›―0―‹+›―‹

Elroy Lindaas was kind enough to send me his schedule of barn dances for this summer. It reminded me of the passing of an old friend, a patron of the dances, about whom I once wrote with affection, and who is fondly remembered now by many. Here is what I wrote about him.

Elmer lives for the butterfly. He is not much for the skip-kick steps of the verses, but when it comes time to figure-eight two women through the chorus, the years fall away, and he skims the polished plywood dance floor like a hovercraft.

I suppose the day will come when, like Elmer, I will be unable to hike ten miles across the Coteau after sharptails, or snowshoe the cattail marshes of winter, or even dig my own spuds, but now I know I will still be able to hitch a ride to the Lindaas Barn Dance for some low-impact polkas and maybe even a butterfly.

That will be important as life, because unlike most Lutherans (St. Paul has a lot to answer for) and most writers (so does Kathleen Norris), I never have considered life on the plains to be an ascetic denial of sensuality. The plains are a place for full play of the senses.

So now, in high summer on the northern plains, open up. Riding in an open vehicle helps, which is what we did one night en route to the old Ladbury Church west of Sibley. This is the church a bunch of us saved from collapse and restored as a community center. George Amann, from over Dazey way, bless his heart, suggested we might run a little lecture series in the church, and it went well.

I particularly enjoyed the heat in the church, and then the dry west breeze as we stepped back outside. That was when I thought about the sublime smells of haying that had washed over me all the way there. I thought, too, of the spidery lavender bergamot blooming up the slopes of the coulees of the Sheyenne, and imagined that its minty scent also had touched me on the road. I know the aroma of white and yellow sweet clover was downright close.

Departing Sibley, and after a quick beverage at Rock'n Rodney's of Luverne, we drove toward Mayville, where I knew Elroy Lindaas already was fronting the band up in his loft. The breeze stilled, and the slough-smell of decay hung heavy. However rotten this smell may be in July, it is not the smell of death; it is the smell of life. Cycles of life spin swiftly during these long days.

So swiftly, and so much is humankind a part of the pace of summer here, that there is just too much life to apprehend it all. I have already missed the Buffalo Shuffle, I realized, and I do not see how I can make it to the Luverne Picnic or to Dazey Days.

We got to the Lindaas Barn Dance and noticed the crowd was a little less than usual, but we then found out that was because there were dances the same night in both Mayville and Portland. I tell you, the pace of summer around here is killing me. Throw me into the slough.

All creatures great and small, we are part of this lively tempo of northern summer. Our festivals and frolics and fairs in our little country towns, pell-mell one upon another, are renewals of community and humanity just as surely as the rotting of sloughs and the raising of broods and the nurture of crops are renewals of nature and the land. There is much to be done in short time. After that we fatten up for winter. Fall supper season, you know.

The last Lindaas Barn Dance of Indian summer marks a change in pace. Winter nears. Deep in hibernation, Elmer and I will dream of the butterfly.

6. THE ROADS ARE PINK RIBBONS

Wherein the prairie historian considers the lilies of the field

Suddenly in September 2008 a lot of people were asking, Where the heck is Sims, North Dakota? The reason was that the White House had announced First Lady Laura Bush would visit the Sims Scandinavian Lutheran Church and Parsonage on Thursday, October 2. Sims is a ghost town in Morton County, but the parishioners of Sims Lutheran not only have kept up their church but also have done a splendid restoration of their white-stucco parsonage.

You have to love these little stories of American democracy. It turns out the good folks in Sims were assisted in their restoration efforts by the state historic preservation organization. Preservation North Dakota made a grant for materials and also brought volunteer restoration workers to the site — my Suzzanne and I among them— rallied by the charismatic director of PND, Dale Bentley. The grant money, though, ultimately traced back to the federal Save America's Treasures program. Mrs. Bush was coming to Sims, then, to acknowledge not only the spirit and labor of local people but also the federal role in historic preservation.

Sims once was a thriving prairie town. It was the creation of the Northern Pacific Coal Company, a subsidiary of the Northern Pacific Railroad, which was attracted to the site by coal deposits in the hills and water supplies from nearby springs. The town got its post office, named for the chief clerk in the Northern Pacific offices, in 1880 and was platted in 1883.

The arrival of the railroad in turn brought farming settlers, mostly Norwegian Lutherans, who made Sims their trade center. In addition, the town had a thriving brickyard. Its population peaked at almost two thousand—but it also declined fast. By 1917, Sims

Sims Lutheran Church awaits First Lady Laura Bush

had only fifty citizens. In 1948 the NP tracks were torn up, leaving behind a concrete bridge across Sims Creek.

There were still Norwegian farmers in the countryside, though, and they kept the Lutheran church alive. In fact they built the parsonage before the church, with the first pastor taking up residence in it in July 1885, and holding services on the second floor. The wood-frame church itself was not completed and dedicated until 1900. Both the church and the parsonage are listed on the National Register of Historic Places.

Now for the ghost, known as the Gray Lady, which is what everybody seems to want to talk about in relation to Sims. It is all a little vague, but evidently in the late 1910s, Bertha Dordal, the church organist and wife of Reverend L. D. Dordal, died in the parsonage. The good reverend then remarried following what seemed an inordinately brief period of mourning. He and his new wife left, but the story goes that Bertha remained, a spirit making her presence known in routine ghostly ways to later residents of the parsonage.

I am not much worried about the Gray Lady, but I would keep an eye on the flesh-and-blood live ladies of Sims Lutheran. They have a history of many good and charitable works and also of being, shall we say, assertive. The minutes of a congregational meeting in 1898 record an addendum stating that "the decisions of someone, especially the Ladies Aid or other intruder person shall hereafter be considered nul[l] and void." Would you not love to know what that was all about? Anyway, in 1920 the men caved and passed a resolution granting equal voting rights to women.

Those Sims Lutheran ladies seem so nice! Looking forward to the big day on October 2, I was sure Mrs. Bush would get a lovely lunch, as well as some conversation rather different from the usual sort of chatter in Washington.

T he Gray Lady, ghost of the Sims Scandinavian Lutheran Church parsonage, was a harmless spirit, says Carol Samuelson. A pastor's daughter who grew up in the parsonage, Carol recalls that the ghost drew water from the hand pump and, when present in the living room, caused the temperature to drop.

"She was very friendly," Carol insists. "It was comforting to have her there." From the chilled living room they would see her ascending the stairs to her bedroom like "the tail end of a cloud."

The day when First Lady Laura Bush came to Sims, she did not see the Gray Lady, but Carol told her about the apparition. Mrs. Bush had just a bite or two of Norwegian almond cake (courtesy of the baker, Annika Nelson) and chatted with people at the potluck in the church basement. Things did not go exactly as planned, but they went well indeed.

The idea behind the First Lady's visit to the ghost town of Sims was to express her support for the Save America's Treasures program, of which she was honorary chairwoman. The Save America's Treasures program had provided funding to the organization, Preservation North Dakota, for restoration of historic buildings, including the historic church parsonage at Sims. Mrs. Bush followed the money to Sims, but also honored the local parishioners, like Donna and Joel Johnson, who worked so hard to restore the place.

Although I am going on to talk about the homely spectacle of the First Lady coming to this little country church, let us remember that the event was, at heart, about the people of Sims Lutheran, who did honor to themselves and to America by restoring this treasure house of the American prairies. They are good people who did a good thing.

As Mrs. Bush did a good thing by coming here. It was interesting to observe the dynamics of the visitation. Attendees were vetted, screened, and selected by White House staff and security. Only about twenty-five church parishioners and a handful of Preservation North Dakota officers were permitted to partake.

On the scene, even in cozy little Sims on a sunlit Indian summer day, security trumped all other considerations. White House staff, mainly in the person of a firm but tactful woman named Christina, had been on the scene for days and had worked out the choreography for the event. When the First Lady drove up, people were supposed to be singing in the church sanctuary, so that the music spilling from the open windows would welcome Mrs. Bush as she drove up on the sunny south side of the church.

When the suits, by which I mean the traditionally black-clad secret service, arrived with the First Lady, they nixed the Norman-Rockwell hymn-singing scene. I am rather sure what happened was they scanned the unsecured ridges all around and said, we are not walking the First Lady around the road here. Instead they took her right to the parsonage for a tour; she was first welcomed officially there by my Suzzanne, a matter of considerable excitement and wardrobe discussion in our household.

Yes, the First Lady did sit down with us in the church basement. We had been instructed to eat slowly, not an easy thing for country people, so we would still have food on our plates when she arrived. She chatted charmingly with us, even seemed to relax a bit. Seated by the oldest member of the church, Ruth Olien, I watched to make sure she turned around in time to grasp the hand of Mrs. Bush before she left.

There was singing after all, for as the First Lady rose to depart, a spontaneous chorus of "God Bless America" welled up, and I saw tears welling, too, in the eyes of the practical women presiding over the kitchen. Mrs. Bush exited the basement walking under an inscription neatly lettered blue on the white plaster, which reads, "With God all things are possible."

Now, a personal postscript. Suzzanne, an officer in Preservation North Dakota, had been selected to greet Mrs. Bush officially on entry into the parsonage. I am pretty sure the rationale for her selection was that people who knew her were confident she would not get tongue-tied but would be able to express a creditable welcome and appreciation when faced with the First Lady of the republic.

What they did not know was that Mrs. Bush, a former librarian and teacher, was a personal hero to Suzzanne. As we prepared to depart our home in West Fargo, there was a wardrobe crisis, as the official greeter had six or eight outfits laid out on the bed and was unable to decide which one was right for the occasion. I finally said just pack them all, she could dress at our hotel in Bismarck, and I lugged her bulging suitcase to the truck.

Of course she performed wonderfully when the time came, and then she wound down during the basement potluck. Suddenly an apparent situation loomed, as one of those black-suited men came to our table, took her by the arm, and said you need to come with me right away.

Where he took her was outside onto the sunlit scoria road, to stand there with Mrs. Bush for a personal photo shoot by the White House photographer. The First Lady had chosen a rose suit for the occasion, Suzzanne a blue one, and there they stood, in colors perfectly suited to the red road and the blue sky. It is not the colors, however, but the associations that make our print of that day's photo a treasured item in our household.

⊳⋅⊷⋅०⋅⊶⋅⊰

Since my arrival in North Dakota in 1992, I have had a steadily increasing involvement in historic preservation — surveying heritage resources in communities and regions of the state, identifying significant sites, nominating historic properties to the National Register of Historic Places, teaching field courses on historic earthen buildings, investing time, sweat, and treasure in works of restoration. It quickly became evident that historic preservation in the wide open spaces of the northern plains was a different game than in many other parts of the country. As recounted in the previous chapter, this is a declensionist country — a place where the threats to historic properties are more often atrophy and neglect than wrecking balls. People and capital are thin on the land, resulting in maintenance deferred. Restoration efforts aimed at overcoming the resulting decay are poorly resourced.

On the other hand, the joys of this type of work are great. Because scholars and preservationists are few and new, there are great opportunities for discovery, for telling the stories of a rich material legacy in a neglected region. There develops a heartening camaraderie among those committed to conserving our cultural legacy, a spirit expressed not only in words but also in acts, often involving hammers and shovels. The work, too, brings contact with all manner of everyday people on the land whom it is a privilege to get to know.

Still, you have to wonder, as the regional economy and society wax and, more often, wane, will it amount to anything? I know there are many skeptics who say, "What is the use?" We cannot serve posterity; we have to look out for ourselves; let the dead bury their dead.

All right then, presume the skeptics are correct. Are they happy, therefore, living in their declensionist world of futility? Because those of us on side with cultural conservation, we are happy, enjoying the company and all the social and sensual experiences of our labors. I think we are better off forging ahead in our delusion that preservation matters, that posterity matters, blooming like lilies. You of little faith, your world and welcome to it.

⊱──◈──⊰

A murmur rippled through the pews of St. Andrew's Lutheran Church, and some of the attendees in the packed country church laughed out loud. "It's a dog," they were saying, "Where did he come from?"

Unfortunately, I can answer that. It was our Labrador retriever, Arnie, who was deathly afraid of thunderstorms. With black clouds looming, and thunder beginning to roll across the Missouri Coteau, he had escaped confinement in our truck and come looking for Mom — right up the center aisle of St. Andrew's.

The event crashed by our willful retriever was Christmas in July, a fundraiser for St. Andrew's, a parish of Germans from Russia in southern McIntosh County. This is one of our prairie churches listed on the National Register of Historic Places, and in fact, it is a twofer — which is to say, it has two church buildings, the 1893 stone-and-clay church as well as the 1906 wood-frame church, both listed.

That summer of 2011 the 1906 church got a new roof, thanks partly to a grant from Preservation North Dakota, and the more so to the members and friends of the parish who raised the matching funds. Christmas in July was their brainchild, and we were invited to the event courtesy of Carol Just, a daughter of the parish. It was worth the drive out just to hear the St. Andrew's Centennial Choir, decked out in red and black, sing the old hymns again in tones innocent of formal training but schooled in prairie experience. When Arnie padded up the aisle, he just added a little humor to the august proceedings.

The wood-frame church dates from the time when most of the more impressive churches on the northern plains were constructed. They were the houses built by faith and wheat, for just as various ethnic immigrant farmers were getting well established in the new land, they benefited from a strong agricultural economy in the first decade of the twentieth century. It is fine to see the 1906 church getting the care it deserves.

The 1893 church is more distinctive, however, and perhaps even unique. I know of no other church building of this kind still standing. It was built by ordinary people, German-Russian farmers, using materials at hand and building in the only style they knew, just the way they built their houses, here or in the old country. They hauled stone from a deposit about twelve miles away and laid it up with mortar of clay — no concrete or lime or other additive, just good old gumbo. I do not know what they plastered it with, but I would not be surprised if some cow manure was involved. Today the walls are covered with concrete stucco and whitewashed.

The old church at the time needed some repair, mainly in a couple of places where the concrete stucco had pulled loose, and some dripboards needed to be replaced. Moreover, some years ago the *Vorheisel*, or entryway, was removed, and so the area around the front door needed some stabilization, perhaps by restoring the Vorheisel. Otherwise, the old church was in great shape, and since 2011, most of the needed repairs have been done. The parishioners are committed to its restoration and preservation, so it should be around as a heritage resource for the region for a long time.

It is quiet sitting inside the old church, the cool interior en-wrapped by walls two feet thick, sunlight streaming through the deep window wells. You can look out over the green cemetery and think about the stories of the people lying there. And there is a yellow dog looking in the window.

~ ⦁ ⦿ ⦁ ~

I t is a guy thing, in my observation. It gets bigger as the years go by. Old guys gather iron like magnets, and they like to put it out there where people can see it.

For many years the best known of these iron men was W. O. Krumwiede, of Voltaire, North Dakota. I used to love to drive Highway 52 up toward Velva and see Bill's vast collection of stationary separators, that is, old-time threshing machines, exhibited on a hillside. Rumely Bill, as people called him, passed away in 2007. His collection was dispersed—I do not know the details of that.

Rumely Bill's obituary said, "W. O. collected antiques, guns, Rumely Oil Pulls, John Deere tractors, antique cars, and traps. Every summer and fall he enjoyed traveling to many of the area and regional threshing shows. He was an avid reader of western novels. W.

O. was known by several nicknames, including Rumely Bill, Trapper Bill, and Bill the Gun Trader."

Rumely Bill was preceded in death by another great iron man, John G. Grenz, known to his many friends as Custer. The difference is that following Custer Grenz's passing in the year 2000, his family preserved his collection as a folk monument and invited the public to enjoy it.

As you drive Highway 34 just east of Napoleon, look for the billboard that reads, "Dinosaurs of the Prairie." Up the fencerow and into the pasture, stretching north up the hillside, is a long line of threshing machines, the collection of Custer Grenz. A little swinging gate invites entrance and a stroll up the hill through history.

German-Russian farmer Grenz was born in 1917, grew up in Napoleon, and married Irene Wittmier in 1942. They farmed on the Streeter Flat and later ran a café in Napoleon. Besides collecting machines, Custer fed his historical sensibility by writing articles for the *Napoleon Homestead.*

His obituary said, "He was an avid antique collector over the years attending most auctions in the tri-state area. He had a special interest in threshing machines and his collection graced the hills three miles east of Napoleon for many years." It still does.

A few years ago the Great Plains archeologist Raymond Wood wrote a spoof piece about the prairie dinosaurs, which he named *Threshersaurus dakotaensis,* wherein he mused about the anthropological significance of such installations as Custer Grenz's Dinosaurs of the Prairie. I think there is an interesting study in human development psychology to be done in order to get at the origins of this guy thing.

Here, however, is another approach to the Dinosaurs of the Prairie: just get out there and enjoy them. You are invited to hike up the hill alongside Custer's prizes, to contemplate the countryside from the ridge, and just to absorb the sensory experience, preferably around dusk.

Dinosaurs on the Prairie, Logan County, North Dakota

Which is what we did, along with four grandkids and a beagle, one summer evening. The beagle flushed critters from beneath the machines, and the kids raced about thinking I have no idea what, but clearly enchanted with the place. I tried not to spoil things with a history lecture. These things speak for themselves.

⊱─•◦•─◦•─⊰

Look left as you turn south from the Almont interchange of I-94, and you will see a specimen of Great Plains architecture that deserves some explanation. It may not get a lot of people excited, but it is one of those structures that says a lot about how we live with the land.

I am talking about a pit silo. Not a trench silo, which is an elongate cut in the ground filled with fermenting forage, but a pit silo, a cylinder excavated and formed into the earth. Think of a vertical cylindrical silo, the kind you see on sentimental calendars, only it is dug into the ground instead of towering above ground.

Pit silos were fairly common from Texas to Saskatchewan, and in North Dakota, county agents particularly encouraged them. This was mainly in the West River country, where agents built and loaned wooden forms for pouring concrete.

This silo at the Almont interchange is different in a couple of ways. First, it is a partial pit model, that is, half below ground, half above. Second, it is constructed of ceramic drainage tile, a common material used for constructing farm buildings from about 1920 on.

The obvious advantage of a partial pit silo was you only had to dig half as deep. It also was somewhat safer than a full pit. Thirty feet down, gas could accumulate and overcome someone at the bottom of the hole. If you fell into a partial pit, it was only a fifteen-foot drop.

This pit silo at the Almont interchange is pretty big, about fifteen feet in diameter. Like other substantial silos, it expresses faith in the country in general — it constitutes physical evidence of confidence in the future — as well as faith in animal husbandry in particular. Such a structure expresses a vision for the land.

As you drive south along the Almont road, you come to a couple of other partial pit silos that go beyond an economic vision. They are, aesthetically, exquisite structures, works of art designed to hold forage. They are constructed of drainage tile, but atop each one is the most beautiful conical roof artfully covered with poured concrete.

One of these silos is a leaning tower, which may not last much longer. The other, about a half-mile away, stands perfectly plumb, and is the home of an impressive flock of pigeons. Each is the remnant structure on an abandoned farm site. I suspect they were constructed by a traveling contractor, and if we were to discover his itinerary, we could follow his legacy across the countryside.

Examine the details, and you see that the builder laid up the tiles to stand lengthways in courses to make the walls. When he had reached the desired height, he then laid a course of tiles flat. Atop this course he began to set more tiles flat, and leaning in slightly, filling in with concrete. These courses had to have been laid over a period of days, so the concrete could harden before going higher. Round iron hatches were installed in the domed roofs, and a ventilator placed on top. A veneer of concrete made the roof tight.

Was it accidental that these functional structures turned out so beautiful? Did the builder back up from his finished product and admire what he had done? Did he know that he was an artist? Make sport of me if you will, but I believe these beautiful silos belong on the National Register of Historic Places.

⊢⊣◆◦◆⊣⊢

Here comes the FedEx man up the drive, and I know what is in the package: a sheaf of sensual delights, punctuated by tragedy. My inscribed first edition of *Spin Dance*, by Paul Southworth Bliss, has arrived.

I came to know the Paul Southworth Bliss of history, often addressed in his day as Colonel Bliss, on account of his house, or country retreat, in Adams County, North Dakota. He named it the Scoria Lily. Here, in *Spin Dance*, is Bliss's poem, "Scoria Lily," with a footnote explaining how in 1934, when the poet first encountered the night-blooming flower, he took it to O. A. Stevens, the great plantsman at North Dakota Agricultural College, for identification.

This sends me to my copy of the *Handbook of North Dakota Plants*, by Stevens, where I read the entry for *Mentzelia decapetala*, common name Evening Star, also known as Scoria Lily; to be found, Stevens notes, "On buttes in burned, crumpled clay ('scoria'), or on clay slopes, Missouri River westward. . . . Flowers open in evening and resemble a cactus flower."

Call me a sentimental fool, but I say, how cool is this, to imagine Col. Bliss, on his first venture into the West River Country, stopping his car in McKenzie County at dusk to examine and smell — because Bliss refers to the "fragrant nectar" of the blossom — this strange flower, a poem forming in his mind, but what should he call the thing? And passing through Fargo on his way back east, wilted blossoms in hand, seeking out Stevens, him of the great herbarium, to identify the flower. Then after a few years, on building his country home in Adams County, naming it for the sensuous lily.

I am transported, specifically to that pasture in Adams County where the Scoria Lily ranch house still stands. Actually, the garage was built first, because Bliss set his workmen building with an unfamiliar construction technique: rammed earth. They built up the walls with earth packed in layers into forms, put a flat roof on top, and thereafter, when Col. Bliss might come by to check on the progress of his house, at least he had a place to park his car.

That remarkable ranch house of rammed earth, and the tragedy of Col. Bliss's suicide in 1940, I will tell about later, because right now I have in hand this lovely collection of poems, *Spin Dance*. Although Col. Bliss remained a historical stranger to me at the time, he became a literary acquaintance some years ago, by virtue of an introduction by the inveterate bibliophile, the late David Martinson, who commended *Spin Dance* to me on account of Bliss's sense of nature and place.

> Between two meadows that I know
> I walked today as in a trance . . .
> I saw the April wind bend low
> And ask the fallow field to dance.
> Was there ever a dance
> Like the spin dance
> Of the wind
> And the April earth!

That title poem by Bliss originated on April 18, 1934, in a field near Stanley, North Dakota. There followed another great poem of prairie farming beginning, "Sing me a song of the coltered plow," that I cannot help not merely reading, but singing.

Best of all for me, though, is the poem with the one-word title, "Scoria."

> And the roads are pink ribbons
> On the breasts of the hills.
> At sunset the sky is scoria, too:
> And the earth and the heavens
> And the people —
> Are all scoria!

Paul Southworth Bliss was a remarkable man in two ways: because he wrote sublime poetry, much of it inspired by the North Dakota landscape, and because he built an extraordinary house, in Adams County, North Dakota. Both his poetry and his house are pretty much forgotten, but deserve to be discovered, preserved, and appreciated.

A directory of artists in North Dakota and an anthology of creative writing, both published in the 1930s, provide basic biography about Paul Southworth Bliss. Of his many books of poetry three deal substantially with North Dakota, the first of which, *Spin Dance*, is the best. Dr. Lawrence Moe of Metropolitan State University, St. Paul, has written elegantly about Bliss's poetic works. Jim Fuglie has written about Bliss with insight in his weblog, *PrairieBlog*.

Too, I got into touch with a woman of eclectic interests named Irene Hause of Sheridan, Wyoming, who also has a blog, called *Wyoming Woman*. She offers particular insights, from an intriguing source, about the personal life of Bliss the poet.

Bliss was, in many ways, a success story and a renaissance man. A Minnesota boy, he was educated at Hamline and Harvard. His first career was as a newspaper reporter. He joined the army on American entry into the Great War, attained the rank of major, served with distinction, and after discharge, wrote the history of his regiment. Subsequently he entered the profession of social work, until in 1933 he was appointed a field representative of the Federal Emergency Relief Administration, stationed in Williston, North Dakota. A promotion put him in the position of Director of Intake, that is, the man in charge of hiring, for the Works Progress Administration in North Dakota, an important and influential position.

It was said Bliss traveled forty thousand miles across North Dakota on public service, learning the landscape that inspired his poetry. On or near land his mother had acquired in 1910 in Adams County, northeast of Haynes, he built a country home, which he christened the Scoria Lily. This was a house and garage constructed in Moderne style, the walls built up with rammed earth. This is to say, the walls were composed of earth compacted in forms. The flat roof was poured concrete. The fireplace was laid up of petrified wood. The house stood atop a rise in the middle of a pasture. A subsequent owner added an immense embankment of scoria boulders that gives the site a fortified look. The house stands today in a state of dignified partial collapse.

What happened to Colonel Paul Bliss, as he often was addressed? Irene Hause recounts that her mother, a German immigrant woman, was the caregiver for Mrs. Bliss — the mother of Paul, who never married. Paul seems to have been quite close to his mother until he went to work in North Dakota, leaving her in the care of Mrs. Hause. Mrs. Bliss wrote a mimeo memoir, much of which was devoted to her son.

What Mrs. Bliss does not recount is that Paul Bliss committed suicide in a YMCA in Kansas City in 1940. The family never told her this. They would write letters to her as if they were coming from Paul, and Mrs. Hause would have to read the letters to the old mother, maintaining the fiction that her son was still alive.

I do not know the details of the downfall of Paul Bliss. Someday I will discover them. For now, I have his poem, "Badlands Sunrise."

Give me clay
For the building
Of valleys and buttes
Not rock,
For rock cannot be made over,
And worked with.

>-+◦+-◦-+◦+-<

"As far as I'm concerned I was happy there, and I never thought too much about it. We took it for granted."

I had asked Bernice Larson, who raised her family in a sod house in Bowman County, North Dakota, in the 1940s and 1950s, what it was like to live in a sod house in the middle of the twentieth century. Was this a hardship, I wondered? Did she feel deprived? Evidently not.

Ordinarily we think of sod houses as temporary expedients, dwellings laid up to fill residence requirements for homesteads, then replaced with proper frame houses when railroads and sales of the first crops made lumber available. It is interesting and significant that some families deliberately chose to remain in their soddies. They bought window glass, laid down wood floors, plastered the interior walls, stuccoed the exterior, and most importantly, put on a tight roof of wood shakes — and then enjoyed the advantages of earthen insulation against the hard elements of the plains.

Bernice Larson was the daughter of homesteaders, Melvin and Jennie Torpen, from Wisconsin. She grew up, a few miles from her future sod-house home, in a family of three daughters. "I usually helped my dad milk, because the other two girls were in the house," she says. She met her future husband, Clark Larson, at local dances held in barns and homes. She married him in 1940. In 1942 they moved onto a rental farm — the residence of which happened to be a sod house, previously occupied by the owners.

"It was in fairly good shape," Bernice recalls. The main part of the house comprised three rooms — a bedroom on the north side, a dining room on the south side, and a living room in the middle. A coal stove in the wall between the living room and the dining room heated the house and also the water for washing.

Attached to the west side of the house was a wood-frame addition, which served as the kitchen. Outside the kitchen door was a windmill. Bernice lived in the sod house from 1942 to 1960 and never had running water. She did, however, get electricity in 1950.

Bernice repainted the interior, with the living room receiving a coat of ecru. She made curtains and laid rugs on the living room and bedroom floors. The kitchen floor was linoleum. That was where people dropped their boots and coats — "Seems like we always found room — I don't know where!"

The house did get a little cramped as the family grew — four children, the oldest born in 1942, the youngest in 1953. This necessitated folding beds in both the living room and the dining room. Eventually the Larsons moved, not only to get a larger house, but also to buy a farm of their own.

In the meantime, Bernice was not a complainer. "Of course the walls weren't really even," Bernice allows, but, "it was a warm house. It was very nice, because the walls were thick. It was nice and cozy. And I had more company then than I did in later years."

That last sentence is a clue, I think, to why people hold fond memories of sod houses. It may be that sod had its environmental advantages, but recollection of those physical facts is wrapped up with remembrance of the social situation of generations past — lots of kids around, dances, school events, and most of all, gatherings of family and neighbors in the house.

"I had so many relations, and we used to get together," Bernice Larson says. "And my neighbors, we had good neighbors. A lot of visiting, card playing. They brought all their children."

The sod house where Bernice Larson raised her family and played cards with the neighbors still stands, in fair condition, uninhabited. Cattle rubbing is the main agent of its gradual destruction.

⊱━◦━⊰

The sod house stands as the foremost material symbol of pioneer life on the Great Plains of North America. It symbolizes both the humility and the aspirations of the pioneers. The old folksong, "Little Old Sod Shanty on the Claim," bemoans the deprivations of sod house life — the lack of window-glass, the leaky roof, even the coyotes howling outside — but it also foretells better times to come. Soon, we are told, others will come, families will grow up with the country, and people will have proper, wood houses.

By the way, that song, "Little Old Sod Shanty," seems to have one or more alleged authors in every state or province from Kansas to Saskatchewan. Some of this confusion comes from bogus claims by would-be authors, but much of it comes from the practices of frontier photographers. After photographing a sod-house family, photographers liked to print stanzas of "Little Old Sod Shanty" on the back of the photographic card, thereby prompting people to attribute authorship of the song.

We think, as people of the plains, that we know what there is to know about sod houses. They were laid up with pieces of grass-bound sod cut with a grasshopper plow; they were temporary dwellings, used to prove up a homestead claim; and once that use was done, people abandoned their soddies for proper housing.

In fact, many thousands of prairie homes referred to as "sod" were not cut sod, but were constructed of earth using some other technique. Many of these, too, were quite substantial, and not considered temporary. People still live in some of them.

A common type of earth house was one constructed of clay bricks something like adobe, although not of Hispanic tradition.

Germans from Russia considered this a proper house from their old country experience, calling the homemade bricks *batsa*. The Black Sea Germans built thousands of them, and the Mennonites of Kansas and Manitoba built thousands more.

The same people also knew how to form up walls from wet clay with their hands, using the technique known as "puddled earth." This was the same type of construction as what English or Irish folk called "cob." It sounds simple, but it was all free-form, so that an artisan of this technique had to know what he was doing.

Somewhat simpler was the earth-fill form of house favored by Ukrainians, among some others. This began with a rectangle of standing posts set in the ground. The builders then nailed lath, or earlier, saplings, inside and outside the posts, forming a cavity that was filled with clay.

I hope it is not too indelicate to mention that all these builders commonly incorporated a little cow dung into the earth mix. It improved the binding and the insulation.

We should not forget, of course, that the Indians of the plains knew the virtues of earth housing long before whites arrived. The earth lodges of the Pawnee, the Arikara, the Mandan, or the Hidatsa were impressive in bulk and comfortable for occupants.

Earth houses were not necessarily temporary, however. They were not merely pioneer expedients. This makes them objects worthy of more than passing interest.

⊱──◦──⊰

Coming home from our annual NDSU field school on historic earth buildings, I came to reconsider the nature of the enterprise. The school is supposed to be about, well, historic earth buildings, which happen to be situated in the magnificent western North Dakota landscape. More and more, though, the school has come to be about the people associated with the buildings and the landscape, people who partake of the character of the earth.

There are, to begin with, the historic personages, the home-steaders who cut or mixed the earth into dwellings and, literally, made themselves at home. There are, too, the beautiful students who make the journey with us, and give us hope that the pioneer spirit lives on. Most of all, though, I am talking about the people in place on the land today, each one typical, each one individual, each one a joy to get to know.

When Lois Fink welcomes us into the Grassy Butte post office, a log-and-sod building constructed by a Ukrainian immigrant, it is as though we are meeting Mrs. McKenzie, the original postmistress. She laughs every time I smack my head on the low pine log beams supporting the pole-and-earth roof.

Down the road (Highway 85) at St. Demetrius Ukrainian Catholic Church, Father Taras Miles dispenses knowledge, wisdom, and charity seasoned with wit as he explains the iconography of the St. Demetrius sanctuary and the history of the parish. His able and dedicated deacon, Leonard Kordonowy, free of the regalia by which we know him during Mass, and now attired in jeans and manly foot-wear, leads us out to Ukrainian homestead and village sites.

Ukrainian homestead houses are spectacular buildings con-structed in unmistakable style, but the experience is all the more rich when Deacon Leonard scans the horizon and sketches in the landscape of memory, pausing now and then to instruct the young folks with the wisdom of experience. (Allow me here to join with all the others congratulating the deacon on his twenty-five years of ser-vice at St. Demetrius, as of 2012. I hope the presence of two bishops along with your friends and family, Deacon Leonard, was enough to make you feel how much you are appreciated.)

Lucinda Martin at the Dunn County Historical Museum and Shirley Halvorson at the Mott Gallery of History and Art are so ab-sorbed in their collections that you feel like if someone did not make them go home, they would take up residence and sleep over with the artifacts. Over east of Mott, Jim Stern is always willing to take a little time after work to show off his grandparents' homestead house-barn, with its masterly stonework and gumbo plastering.

(A little sidebar question: What two types of people on the northern plains built homes that brought livestock under the same roof as the people? That would be the native builders of earth lodges, the Mandan, Hidatsa, and Arikara, and the Germans from Russia, as illustrated by the Stern homestead house.)

Landowners like Jim Odermann of Belfield and Lynn Braun of Scranton come out to the field to talk with the students and exchange observations about their historic earth buildings, because they simply are curious about how people built and lived in houses of earth.

I must not fail to mention the Benedictine hospitality that makes it possible for a company of scholars to study and work in western North Dakota during its current economic boom. Brother Michael and the monks of Assumption Abbey welcome us in the spirit of their order. Attendance at vespers with the brothers is an excellent way to center the students for the field school experience. And when Brother Placid Gross strolls over for a chat after vespers, I could listen to him all night, just for the cadence of his speech, which is just as much a product of the earth as the buildings we study.

><+>-O-<+>-<

Following a late-night return from the field school on historic earth buildings, I am thinking this is the way people should see North Dakota, and particularly western North Dakota.

So often tourism is a packaged experience of so-called attractions and engineered hospitality. Even if you plan your own itinerary and travel on your own, it is hard to break free of the usual patterns. When you do, the rewards are great.

Over a span of years Suzzanne and I have taught a summer field school called "Prairie Earth, Prairie Homes." Its focus is historic buildings made of earth. Right away you think of sod, meaning cut sod laid up into walls, but there are many ways of building with earth, representing many traditions and styles.

Because the earliest earth-building traditions are native, we start at the Knife River Indian Villages. This is a National Park Service site, but you know, you will not find yourself fighting crowds there. Up the road near Dunn Center, to make the point that resource extraction has a long history in these parts—as in about eleven thousand or twelve thousand years—we stop in to see Gail and Allen Lynch at the Knife River flint quarries. This is a private site, just recently designated a national historic landmark by the secretary of the interior. At both of these places your imagination runs free, and you get a sense of the antiquity of life in these parts.

We spend several days working on the historic Hutmacher farm, a German-Russian farmstead of earth-roofed buildings in Dunn County. Here antiquity and modernity mix and sometimes collide, as petroleum development writes a new chapter in the history of regional resource extraction.

Our other travels during the field school make a backlash snarl on the map of western North Dakota. Billings County offers the houses of Ukrainian homesteaders, who built walls of earth in an old-country style unlike any other building tradition on the prairies. German-Russian buildings are everywhere, many of them well-preserved and making adept use of native stone, gumbo clay, and cow manure as materials of construction.

North Dakota has its sod houses, too, commonly built by Anglo-Americans or by Norwegians. One of them stands in the ghost town of Haley, down on Grand River, a place where the past is so present you cannot fail to sense it.

The richness of the region is not confined to historical features, however, and travel across it is all the more flavorful if you take your chances on local cafés, drive-ins, and bar and grills. A modest but well-run establishment like the Poolside Drive-In of Mott was a place not only to stoke up on sloppy burgers but also to observe humanity coming and going; I am sorry it is no longer in business. The Eats N Treats, the drive-in of Bowman, is a regular entrepot, and the soups, especially the creamy ones like the Knoephle or the potato-bacon, are terrific. For a heavy feed, and a full dose of West River kitsch, there is Trapper's Kettle in Belfield. Go ahead, try the borscht.

And now, the pièce de résistance — rhubarb custard pie at the Four Corners Cafe, Fairfield. None better. So, how do you find out about all these heritage sites and watering holes across North Dakota? Just ask, I am not jealous.

⊱•⊰—○—⊱•⊰

Settlers of the Great Plains, as we commonly think, had to make do with what they had. This meant, in the absence of timber, building houses from the earth — from cut sod. Such homes were temporary, of course, until more proper building materials could be acquired.

Or maybe not. The more we find out about the building traditions of the various peoples of the plains, the more we realize that earth was not just a material of last resort. Many plains folk considered houses of earth — cut sod, earth brick, or other forms of earth construction — to be perfectly proper residences and suited to the country.

Not only that, it gets even more earthy than earth. I mean, large groups of settlers considered cow manure an essential building material.

German Mennonite settlers in Kansas, Manitoba, and elsewhere on the prairies laid up house walls of earth brick commonly known as *Batsa*. This was rather similar to the Hispanic tradition of adobe. The Mennonite builders wet-mixed clay, straw, and manure and packed it into wooden forms. After sun-drying, the bricks were laid up three courses thick, making a strong, well-insulated wall. The manure not only acted as a binder in the mix but also provided an insulating factor. Think about the texture of a dried cowpie, and you will realize how it would help retain energy that would pass right through a hard, clay brick.

Other Germans from Russia, as well as Ukrainians, brought their own traditions of building, and particularly plastering, with manure. From personal examination, I would say that the Ukrainians were the masters of manure plastering. It is possible they added some lime or wheat paste to mix, I am not sure, but I do know that their manure-plaster finishes were creamy-smooth. In house interiors they were painted or papered. It seems oil-based paints adhered nicely.

For many years I have been involved with a group that is restoring a German-Russian farm site, the historic Hutmacher farm in Dunn County, North Dakota. I have been insisting all along that we need to make more use of manure. We had a paid consultant who did not like the idea. When we had Eleanor Hutmacher, who grew up on the place, out to visit with our restoration crew, I took the opportunity to ask her specifically about this matter.

Eleanor described in detail how she and her sister were required to mix, with bare feet, the plaster mix her father smeared on the house and outbuildings. It was a combination of clay, straw, and cow manure.

So we gave it a try, although we did the mixing in wheelbarrows with hoes. Fortunately we had access to high-quality, smart manure from a university ranch nearby, stuff already mingled with pulverized hay by the cattle hooves. It mixed up nicely with clay we mined from the pit out back of the buildings we are restoring. It went on the walls and adhered just fine, a successful experiment. Our field school students, including some stylish co-eds, were great sports about working with this material.

The experiment presented us with a naming opportunity. At first there were various coarse phrases used to describe our material, until "poo-plaster" emerged as the accepted term. Then, in a stroke of promotional genius, someone coined the phrase, "prairie plaster." So prairie plaster it is, in public utterances. As with so many matters of public relations, when you get right down to it, it is still cow manure.

⊱┈•✦•┈○┈•✦•┈⊰

In the course of our travels with the NDSU field school on historic earth buildings, we have become more and more fond of Billings County and its Ukrainian culture region.

The features and contours of this region are not well known, despite heavy traffic. People stream through it via Highway 85, shuttling between the north and south units of Theodore Roosevelt National Park, or bustling to work sites in the oil patch, and remain unaware of its cultural distinctiveness. Nowadays you better keep moving right along, because with the petroleum boom, and with the northern reaches of Highway 22 sometimes closed by mudslides, Highway 85 is like an urban freeway compressed into two lanes.

Because we are looking for historic buildings, though, we pull off and find things not to be seen anywhere else across the state. Ukrainian immigrants arrived here and took homesteads during the first decade of the twentieth century. As they commenced their improvements, including both residences and outbuildings, they built in old country style, using a mix of earth and timber.

A Ukrainian home builder first trekked over west to the Badlands and cut some cedar posts. These posts then were set vertical into the ground to outline a building. Horizontal lath, or in some cases sticks of brush, perhaps split in half, were nailed up and down the posts. Then the cavity between the lath was filled from above with a mix of gumbo clay and manure and straw, producing a wall supported by the posts and insulated by the earth.

The classic Ukrainian house had two rooms, which could be quite commodious. If built in true old-country style, it had a distinctively belled hip roof.

Many of these Ukrainian homestead buildings still stand, most of them in some state of decay, a few still inhabited. Land patent files reveal there used to be many more of them, including barns as long as sixty feet, constructed of posts and clay.

Our interest in this Ukrainian culture region is heightened by our acquaintance with Father Taras Miles, the priest of the Ukrainian Catholic churches in Belfield and Fairfield. The latter is a country church, St. Demetrius, where we had the pleasure of attending Mass.

This was an experience to be savored (although I am sure my Missouri Synod Lutheran grandmother was rolling in her grave). Arriving early, we heard women in the choir loft repeating the rosary, a comforting drone over the sanctuary that centered attendees for the service to follow. Father Miles explained to us that the Ukrainian Catholic Mass is a "sensate experience," and we should just "let it happen." He was right, as our attempts to follow the liturgy soon were stymied by our lack of Ukrainian language skills and by the mysteries of the faith. Of course, mystery is a fine thing, and faith is a mystery not only to outsiders but also, perhaps especially, to adherents.

The choir, mostly male, was wonderful. How just five guys can produce such sound is another mystery of the faith. Four-part harmony, parallel thirds, unison singing, octaves, they filled the church.

After Mass it was up the road to the Four Corners Cafe for dinner with Father Miles and with Deacon Leonard, his wife Laverne, and their great-granddaughter Stephanie. I will not talk again about the rhubarb custard pie served by Stephanie Klym at Four Corners. Oh the heck I won't!

It is just one of the things that bring us back to Billings County again and again.

＞┄◆＞┈◎┄◆┄┈◄

A sensate experience, Father Miles called the Ukrainian Catholic Mass, full of sights, scents, and voices. There is a literary trope as to life on the plains, one that parallels the declensionist narrative in history. It is a trope famously expressed by Kathleen Norris in her extended essay, *Dakota: A Spiritual Geography*, a work in which I delight but do not concur. Norris portrays the plains as a place of monastic asceticism, even deprivation, that makes us spiritually better, maybe even poetic. It seems to me that our monks in this part of the country are mostly Benedictines, who are not into deprivation. The fellows at Richardton raise a prodigious garden and eat well from it, in a dining room with a spectacular view of the landscape yawning to the north. Neither they nor I think of this as a place to starve yourself of sensate satisfactions.

To spend time with material antiquities, to travel the land in search of them, to lay up rock and mix gumbo mortar, with even a little cow shit for seasoning, to get dirty, sweaty, and hungry in your work, then come in for refreshment — was there ever a spin dance like this?

7. AUTUMN'S RARE AND GLORIOUS DAYS

In which the prairie historian talks with his mouth full

Call me ghoulish, but on arriving in a new place, I like to have a look around the cemetery to see what sort of folk I am dealing with. So on arrival at Nora Lutheran Church to attend the annual lutefisk and meatball dinner, first we confirmed (by evidence of the Honeruds, Ohnstads, and Tollefsruds here at rest) the Norwegian credentials of the congregation. Then, squinting through the golden glare of Indian summer and the thirty-mile-per-hour wind, we wondered, what is that trailer doing backed up in the rear of the parish hall?

The answer is, that is how lutefisk happens these days. There are, in fact, lutefisk contractors who supply the product, know how to prepare it, and act as impresarios for events such as this.

Now I know what you are thinking — if there is a small cadre of fellows perpetuating the practice, and lodges and churches are dependent on them, then by getting rid of just a few people, say by buying them out and bribing them to move to Florida, we could banish lutefisk from the land. If that is what you are thinking, then it is because of a bad lutefisk experience. Really, lutefisk prepared under the tutelage of these specialists is pretty palatable. Give it a chance.

Or you may be thinking, if lutefisk comes from experts, then it is not folkloristic enough for you. You would like it prepared, perhaps, by little old Nordic ladies shuffling around the parish kitchen and maybe tut-tutting a little bit and acting matronly. Well, grow up.

Realize that what is happening is ethnic tradition in a new phase with an integrity of its own. There is a role in any community for specialists charged with the preservation of tradition. The iron cross maker of a German-Russian community, for instance, or the separator man of a threshing ring, or a midwife — such people possess skills others need not learn, and they hold them in trust for the people.

That was the role we found Warren Melby playing in the trailer. He supervised the work of John Reierson and others of the congregation poaching the chunks of lutefisk (seven minutes, then figure it cooks a little more in the pan en route to the tables, coming out just right). This is the culmination of three days of preparation, salting and rinsing the preserved cod, then cutting it up in a joint effort that in John's recounting sounds appealing: "A bunch of guys outdoors talking and telling stories." Inside the hall we find the other specialist, Carrol Juven, anchoring kitchen operations. "It's a labor of love," he says.

Recognize, too, that although we may love to make fun of lutefisk, it is an acquired taste, and once acquired, it is compelling — no doubt because of its sensual capacity to evoke remembrance, but also because people really like it. The fellow beside me at the table, on my right elbow, did not regard lutefisk as an ethnic duty to be consumed ritually and reluctantly. He filled his plate with a double portion of lutefisk three times — six portions of lutefisk! And the fellow on my left, there he sat with his plate filled, and as he waited for the pitcher of melted butter to slather it with, he visibly trembled with anticipation.

The dinner at Nora Lutheran is nicely done in many ways, including the waiters kitted out in black slacks and white shirts and bowties. The meatballs, too — I conversed with Harlan Swenson, CEO of the congregational meatball enterprise. He talked about the right proportions of beef and pork and onions, about precooking on outdoor grills, and about the nutmeg and allspice in the gravy.

It was Don Reierson who invited us out for the dinner, and it was he, I am told, who put that jig-cut fish-sign with the legend, "LUTEFISK," at the Gardner exit. Red-mouthed, the stiff fish beckoned, seductively. We followed.

⋈⋯◆⋯○⋯◆⋯⋈

The institution of the fall supper on the northern plains seals the connection between the seasons and the senses. It is, after all, a *fall* supper, celebrating a season that in this country is delightful, fruitful, and ominous. It is, for both preparers and diners, full of sensory triggers of memory — sage, kraut, cod — scents that stir remembrance and cement relationships. Diners traveling to a supper traverse a prairie landscape at its best, golden and mellow. The preparation of food, the choreography of kitchen, the organization of service all are matters of ritual. The ritual is a homily, admonishing us to eat well, live well, connect with our neighbors, and appreciate the bounty and beauty of the land.

The fall supper also serves as an exemplar. Heed the homily. Throughout the year, explore the potential of the seasons, the land, the community, and what they all, in combination, offer to the faithful and the adventurous.

><∙∘∙<

We think of them as local matters, as our own affairs, these fall feeds taking place in our churches — laboring in home and church kitchens, gathering people together, generating a little congregational revenue before winter sets in. We do not stop to think that we are part of something big, something that unites us in ritual up and down the plains. The fall supper is too humble an observance to inspire big pictures.

Perhaps it should, though. I grew up with this custom, specifically with the annual fish fry at St. John's Lutheran Church, Ellinwood, Kansas. Later I greatly enjoyed the fall feeds at St. Joseph's Catholic Church in Olpe, Kansas — meals featuring turkey and sauerkraut, a combination of which I will say more later.

Common on the southern plains, the fall supper ritual is much more predominant, pervasive, as you go north. Every northern plains café or gas station is full of homely autumn notices as to which church is serving what and when. No other part of the plains can outstrip the Canadian prairies in presentation of the fall platter. I challenge anyone, though, to show me a better fall supper than the annual turkey and kraut supper at St. Mary's Catholic Church, Dazey, North Dakota. On an October night I recall I arrived late and got in with the last sitting in the church basement, but there was still plenty of food. (St. Mary's follows the common practice in this part of the country of seating people in the pews to wait, then bringing them into the dining area in platoons.)

This, friends, is kraut the way it is supposed to be. The women of the Ladies Aid, along with some of their men, gather on the last Saturday in August to cut about 350 pounds of cabbage. The women cut, and the men crush the cabbage with their fists into big plastic garbage cans. These are sealed with plastic bags filled with water sitting atop the cabbage.

After that, says Peggy Wieland, who is telling me about it in the church kitchen, "We don't touch it. And you know what, it's never failed." At which point another voice sang out from the kitchen crowd, "Tell 'em about all that German sweat that goes in it!"

I do not know about the sweat, but on the day of the church supper, the first Saturday in October every year, the cooks assemble again and cook the kraut along with about eleven pounds of onions. They cut chunks of roast pork into it, and thicken it with flour and water, so that the serving consistency is creamy. Norm Erber of Oriska, a renowned local caterer, does the turkeys. Parish women bring in pies and dressing. Potatoes and gravy are done at the church.

The fall supper custom at St. Mary's, although there were certain chronological gaps, goes back further than current participants can remember. Mary Wieland, who married into the parish in 1942, says it already had been going for a long time then. She thinks it may have originated in order to help pay for the new church, built in 1929. (A church, incidentally, that is among the most lovely on the plains, a stunning, stucco structure.)

"Years ago the ladies each brought sauerkraut from home, along with three chickens, a gallon or so of peeled potatoes, pies, and so on," Mrs. Wieland recalls.

I was diner number 562. I will be back. In fact, I decided I would like to go out and help cut kraut, if the ladies would let a Lutheran take a turn smashing cabbage.

><+>-0-<+<

The first trees came from the Sheyenne River bottom, dug up and replanted here in this holy site by Jacob Wieland. Now row upon row encloses the stucco St. Mary's Catholic Church, between Sibley and Dazey, and shades its annual Corpus Christi procession. It is a striking effect to drive in from the sunflower fields of golden autumn, enter the sheltered church grounds, and then descend to the church basement.

Which is what I did on a late August Saturday, coming to share, by the kind invitation of Peggy Wieland, in the annual cabbage cutting day at St. Mary's. It is a ritual that precedes by about one month the St. Mary's Fall Supper, which features turkey and kraut. I had attended the supper the previous year, and it was great. You never tasted better kraut.

It begins here and now with 350 pounds of cabbage and an experienced crew of church volunteers. It used to be just about all women, I hear, but now it is men and women and girls and boys.

Five sit at the serving counter and begin the processing of cabbage heads — removing outer leaves (saving some of them for a purpose to come) and quartering. The quarters pass to the kitchen island counter and thence into the hands of four individuals operating old-fashioned wooden kraut cutters, generally bought at farm sales.

The big bowls of shredded cabbage go next to Peggy, who does the salting. Again and again she fills a two-quart measure with cabbage, then adds a spoonful of salt. Alternate measures go into each of two large rubber trash containers. Bent over each are two people punching away at the cabbage to get the juice flowing. Now and then they dip the excess juice, looking like pale sea-foam, into a bucket, so that the cabbage will compact properly.

This goes on for a couple of hours, until the cabbage is all in the cans. Then, while some visit and have coffee and rolls, others finish the process by sealing the containers. The juice is poured back in. The clean outer leaves are laid on top; there is going to be some spoilage, and these leaves will be no loss.

Then comes the stroke of folk genius. Double garbage bags are placed atop the cabbage leaves and filled, slowly, with a water hose. They expand to cover the tops of the cans and seal them completely. The kraut cans are left undisturbed in the church basement until the

Cutting kraut at St. Mary's Catholic Church, Barnes County, North Dakota

day before the fall supper, about a month later. The method never fails — perfect kraut every time. The fall supper comes on the first Sunday in October. Saturday is the day the volunteers show up to cook the kraut. They fry onions in lard, add the kraut to the big pots, and thicken with flour and water. Finally, they add chunks of pork, roasted separately.

This is impressive. And yet it is only one current manifestation of a rich cultural life in this parish, formed by Schwabian German immigrants in the 1890s. They built their frame church in 1904 and this marvelous stucco church in 1929. They have celebrated Corpus Christi since 1906. Early celebrations featured a male choir and a brass band performing such original compositions as John Wieland's "St. Mary's Parade March." Here in the basement, Joe

Berger tells me, "We used to put on three-act plays." John Amann organized these and directed.

So often we think of pioneer life as a matter of deprivation and loneliness. This just does not match up with the record of such places as St. Mary's. Pioneer life here had a complex calendar and a vital culture. Cabbage day and the fall supper echo that vitality.

Just imagine the day when Bishop Shanley came to dedicate the church. As told in the county history, "All the men of the parish went to meet the Bishop at the train at Dazey, some on horseback, some with buggies." Can we recapture even a remnant of their exhilaration and camaraderie? Come on, we can try.

———✦—○—✦———

A century ago in Munich, North Dakota, a baby boy of Icelandic descent was named by his parents for the first white European child born in the New World — Snorri Thorfinnson. The boy grew up in North Dakota and among kin in Manitoba. He graduated from North Dakota Agricultural College and went on to a distinguished career as a professional extension worker and an amateur (which term I use with reverence, referring to its Latin root) historian.

Thorfinnson died in 1986 in the community of his retirement, Fort Ransom, North Dakota. He was one of those citizen-historians who went about investing his home country with story and meaning. He was fascinated with Indian antiquities — burial mounds, the Writing Rock — and especially with what he took to be evidence of early Norse presence in the region. Viking mooring stones along the Sheyenne River, for instance.

This sort of mythmaking is easy to parody, and many professional historians such as I would do so, but whereas I may joke about such matters, I will not denigrate them. I see in Snorri Thorfinnson a purity and sincerity that I cannot match, but still may emulate.

I got to thinking about all this while doing the grouse opener, which involved a ten-mile hike through the grand prairie pastures of the Missouri Coteau. My retriever is young, and I am old, so now and then I found a seat on a pile of glacial rock and just contemplated the countryside. I remembered that Snorri, a bird hunter and a sometime-poet (he was Icelandic, after all), once wrote,

> God, help us to appreciate
> Autumn's rare and glorious days.

A rare and glorious day on the Coteau with Angie, the History Dog

Snorri was a Farmers Union man who believed that the changes in our land and the depopulation of the agricultural countryside were not just the work of large, impersonal forces but rather matters of values and choices. Another of his poems was called "Big Operator." In it he wrote of tearing down farmhouses, bulldozing shelterbelts, pulling up fences, all because "I need land, more land, and greater wealth." He predicted that as the farms went, so would the main streets, and of course, the people.

> They'll come and go, no need for school or church
> Nor all the folderol of country life.

Here I sit on a pile of rocks in a cow pasture — hard evidence that this was once a cultivated land, which now has gone back to prairie.

It is a beautiful prairie. A place does not have to be untouched by humankind, or labeled a wilderness, in order to be beautiful. It might be useful, too, and be exquisitely beautiful. Just look about with me at these potholes teeming with waterfowl; at these scarlet bullberries promising winter sustenance, perhaps even grace; and yes, at these happy calves.

There is the possibility in these times of a life on the plains whereby humankind and nature do not do daily battle, but rather meet in daily embrace, complementing one another. I can see this Middle Landscape in my mind, and sometimes with my eyes. Snorri saw it, too, and knew its potent appeal. Snorri wrote of "The Message of the Prairies." "It is not a call to the cities," he averred. He said,

> The wild winds . . .
> . . . tell me of wide, sunlit spaces
> Swept by the Northwind bold,
> Of men who dare face the cutting air
> And live on these prairies cold.

Ah, but today, Snorri, the prairies are not cold. Autumn's rare and glorious days.

>-+-+>--0--<+-+-<

I t is time for a good old-fashioned North Dakota blizzard story, the story of Father Joseph Goiffon and his unfortunate adventures in the Red River Valley in 1860.

Father Goiffon was born in France in 1824 and ordained a priest there in 1852. He arrived in St. Paul, Minnesota, in 1857 and the next year was sent out to assist Father Belcourt at St. Joseph (Walhalla today) and Pembina in what is now northeastern North Dakota. There he ministered to the French, Indian, and Métis residents.

The fall of 1860 Goiffon came back from the autumn buffalo hunt on the plains with the Métis and found himself summoned to St. Paul on church business. He traveled to St. Paul accompanied by two Métis men, Paul and Charles Morneau. After about ten days there, the Morneaus were ready to head home. They wanted to join a larger traveling party from St. Boniface, Fort Garry (now Winnipeg), Manitoba. Father Goiffon, however, protested that it was Sunday.

Thus, Goiffon and the Morneaus started a day later, the priest on a new horse he had bought in St. Paul. They made poor progress across Minnesota because of broken wheels and axles on their Red River carts. When they got to Georgetown, just before crossing the Red River, Father Goiffon rode ahead of the carts to catch up with the men in the St. Boniface party.

Father Goiffon found the St. Boniface men at the crossing of the Big Salt River, passed them, and pushed on toward Pembina. It started to rain, and so, uncertain of the best route, the priest stopped to await the party at what he called the Little Salt River, what we now know as Park River. This was where he got into trouble. It was early November. The weather had been fair, but the priest awoke alongside Park River lying in six inches of snow.

I have to say, Father Goiffon showed some pretty poor judgment. He left the timber along the river and camped on the prairie in a blizzard. He crawled under his buffalo robe and went to sleep. His horse died. When the weather broke and he tried to get up, he found his feet were frozen. Travelers from Pembina found Father Goiffon just in time to save his life. They brought him to the home of Joseph Rolette in Pembina, where he was fed and thawed out.

The bishop then sent a sledge from St. Boniface to fetch him. There were nuns to care for him at St. Boniface, and doctors, too, who concluded his life could be saved only by amputating his rotting feet. They took off his right leg and planned to amputate most of his left foot later.

Before they could perform the second surgery, other emergencies intervened. Some nuns who were heating buffalo tallow to make candles set fire to the bishop's residence. The residence and St. Boniface cathedral both went up in flames. Priests rescued Father Goiffon from the burning house.

Now here comes the legendary part of the story. By the night of the fire, the doctors had given the stricken priest up for dead. He was bleeding from a broken artery in the stump of his right leg. Right after the fire, however, the bleeding stopped. The bishop said it was a miracle. Others said Father Goiffon got so cold when he was carried out that the blood finally clotted. The doctors took off most of his other foot, but Father Goiffon remained an active priest — a few more months at St. Joseph, and then a long life, to 1910, serving parishes in Minnesota.

In 1908 the bishop at St. Boniface dedicated a new and grander cathedral. He invited the aged Father Goiffon to the dedication, and also asked him to write down the story of his survival. That is how we know the story today.

Between dusk and midnight they trail out from the neighbor's grove, leaving their sheltered and snowy bed-grounds. Twenty or thirty whitetails are wintering here. Willow Creek, a snow trap, snakes through the adjacent fields, but on the divides between the bends, bits of crop residue are exposed by the wind, or lie not far beneath the snow. The whitetails rustle meager rations here every night. They make lovely landscape features in the moonlight. The dog considers them a threat to home security, but not so much a threat as to move him to plow out through the snow to investigate. He is monitoring the situation. We go inside and flick on the propane fireplace. The deer return to their cold beds.

I hope they make it. I hope we see these does out with their fawns again next summer, but it is a dicey proposition. Last year bad luck for farmers, resulting in lots of corn left standing in the fields, was good fortune for deer. Not so this year. Pickings are slim in this landscape.

Game and fish authorities say wildlife remains in pretty good shape, so far. They refer mainly to deer. Official observers say pheasants, too, are faring well. I am skeptical on both counts. My correspondents are reporting they never saw so many pheasants in western North Dakota. Which means, I fear, the birds have flocked up in the farmsteads and on the roads and are dependent on grain spillage and silage scraps and kindhearted friends. The more pheasants you see in winter, the worse the conditions in the field.

The Three Tribes at Fort Berthold are ramping up for wildlife winter feeding operations, something they have done for years. One tribal employee has posted a photograph of a good-sized whitetail buck collapsed on the highway from malnutrition. The tribes feed the deer hay partly to divert them from farmers' winter stores, but they also put out seed for pheasants. Some people say this sort of feeding operation is futile or worse, but I disagree. With the congregation of deer and pheasants that takes place in a winter like this, it is quite feasible to make a significant contribution to their survival.

I am not an animal rights person, but I am a lover of animals, and of wildlife. Along with every other sportsman across the region, I contemplate the consequences of the hard winter for hunting next fall. That is not what I think about, though, as I watch my ghostly whitetails pawing the snow across the road. They nudge me, as I stand on the section road, into an attitude of prayer.

I love a living landscape, rich in wild things. The living landscape in the Red River Valley already is imperiled by too many pressures. I have not seen a flickertail gopher since the flood of 1997. Nightcrawlers are few, even after a warm rain. Bobolinks do not nest in Roundup-ready corn. This little herd of whitetails is my personal gauge of the broader predicament of the landscape.

There is also, I admit, a sentimental element to my observation of this survival story. If ever I should cease to have that sort of sentiment, I will know it is time, too, to hang up the shotgun and rifle. Some of you know what I mean, and for those who do not, I am not sure I can explain.

><+>-O-<+-<

Flying home from a couple of weeks abroad, we sort of missed (that is, slept through) the First of Advent. That is too bad, because Advent on the northern plains is so much better than Christmas, if you can keep the Christmas madness from backing up and polluting it.

The hymns of Advent are better than Christmas carols, too. They are hymns of anticipation, of course, but more than that. The Advent hymns are about healing, and promises kept, and, well, grace, which is something you really need when it gets dark at about four o'clock.

I really do not mind it getting dark in the not-so-late afternoon on the northern plains. Seasonality is something to be treasured, and the change of pace that comes with early dark, the opportunity for flickering fires and good books, that is something I welcome. For a month or so, anyway.

Seasons are cultural constructions born of the interaction with environment. Most denizens of western civilization are programmed to think in terms of the conventional four, but how well do these four seasons work in our latitude of a continental region? How often is Thanksgiving a fall feast? How often is Easter a spring event? Cultures innocent of our venerable constructions forge their own seasons. There are aboriginal tribes in Australia who discern seven seasons in the year. We might try reconfiguring the seasonal calendar here.

That may sound confusing, but every one of us suffers from seasonal calendar confusion. I am a farmer, a professor, an outdoorsman, a Lutheran, and a couple of other identities — every one of which has its seasonal demarcations. Trouble is, they overlap, and sometimes conflict.

The true benefit of a religious calendar comes when you allow it to trump the others. Right now I am going a little crazy on account of the academic calendar. Some of my students are more crazy than I am, and they like to share the pain. Let me light the first candle of Advent, then the second, then the third, and things just mellow out. Now back to those Advent hymns. I have an outlaw hymnal. It is the old red hymnal, the Concordia 1941 hymnal, Missouri Synod. The Red One. You can get in a lot of trouble for having one of these red ones, so keep this just between us, all right?

In keeping with the Advent outlaw spirit, my favorite Advent hymn has to be "On Jordan's Bank the Baptist's Cry." This is not a song of supplication. Its verses are imperatives. The one I love best is,

> Lay on the sick Thy healing hand
> And make the fallen strong to stand;
> Show us the glory of Thy face
> Till beauty springs in every place.

I mean, there is no nice please and thank you in that. Good Lord, what are you thinking, anyway? Get to work and heal these people, and pick them up when they need a hand; we are doing what we can here, but You have to do Your part, darn it. And while You are at it, we could use some beauty around here, maybe cover up this ironclad earth with a little fresh snow, how about a pretty sunset for a change, some chickadees and redpolls, how about that?

For Thou art our Salvation, Lord, Our Refuge, and our great Reward, so let us have some of that.

⊱─◈─○─◈─⊰

In early January of 1909, the *Hunter Herald* printed this announcement, one welcome to the citizens of Arthur, North Dakota: "Capt. John McFall and his jolly hunters will entertain Capt. Collins and his merry crowd Friday evening, Jan. 15, with an oyster supper and a dance." Afterward the same paper recounted, "One of the pleasant social functions of the season was the oyster supper and dance given Friday evening by John McFall and his able aid de camp. . . . The best of everything was spread before the guests. . . . Following the supper the dance began and all had a merry time. . . . Not until the strains of Home Sweet Home were played did the crowd commence to disperse." That was well after midnight, I am sure.

In the cluttered calendar of fall food events we see these days, the fish fries and turkey dinners and lutefisk feeds, oyster suppers no longer figure. For plains folk of the late nineteenth century, they were commonplace. In fact, historian Paul Hedron, writing in *Montana Magazine of Western History*, says that oyster suppers "were something of a mania."

When I first began to encounter references to such events in prairie newspapers, I presumed they were talking about canned oysters, but not so! In the nineteenth century oysters were in abundance on the east coast — practically a mandatory item for hors d'oeuvres, and cheap enough for working class people to eat commonly. Out west, people wanted the product, but shipping costs drove up the price so that an oyster supper was considered a special event.

Moreover, the logistics of shipping oysters on ice to the prairies posed certain limitations. I made a search for newspaper references to oyster suppers, and discovered two things, both quite logical. First, oyster suppers prevailed in the states from Kansas north, and second, they took place in the winter, October to February.

Sometimes an oyster supper was a truly elegant event confined to the wealthier citizens of the town. The *Abilene Reflector* of Kansas in 1888 described one such occasion at which, after the oysters, "a few hours were spent over cigars in conversation and amusements." The names of the guests were printed with pride.

In other cases the democratic mass of citizens was invited to partake. In 1882 the Methodists of Dodge City gave an oyster supper in the Ford County courthouse. A similar supper in Nemaha City, Nebraska, in 1899 seemed less likely to be disrupted by exuberant cowboys. "The Methodist Sunday School will give a fresh oyster supper at the Minck Hall Saturday night of this week—December 9," it was announced. "A lunch of cake, pie and coffee will be furnished those who do not want oysters. Proceeds to apply on pastor's salary. Lunch, 10 cents; supper, 15 cents."

Country folk shared the same tastes as townspeople. I read in an 1879 edition of an Iola, Kansas, paper that two gatherings of country people — one over on Deer Creek and the other west of town — had oysters for New Year's. In the latter case the bivalves must have been well lubricated, for as the paper reported, some of the boys afterward "got lost on the prairie and froze some of their toes."

I really doubt any such thing happened following the November 1901 wedding of Miss Mary Jane Goodman and Mr. John Daniel Greene in Sheldon, North Dakota. There the happy couple entered the family parlor, decorated with carnations, to the tune of Mendelsson's wedding march, and after an hour of cordial visiting, "a dainty oyster supper was served."

I am thinking the oyster supper is the sort of winter event ripe for revival in the twenty-first century. Make mine Kilpatrick.

><+>-0-<+><

A pheasant from the freezer is an invitation to experimentation, the way I see it. The ring-necked pheasant is no native, but an introduced bird, an immigrant like most of us people of the plains. Unlike the native grouse, it thrives in an altered plains environment of crops brought from Europe, Asia, and Africa. So when it comes to cooking one, there is no correct, indigenous way. I wish, though, that people would do a better job with it.

The challenge in cooking a pheasant is that it is really two birds. There is the breast, which is rather white meat, only dense in texture and deep in flavor, like chicken on steroids. Then there is the rest of the bird, mainly leg and wing, darker flesh.

The problem is that if you cook the bird long enough so that the breast is done, then the legs and wings are fossilized. That is why pheasants are not good birds for roasting.

The usual solution is some sort of fricassee — cut up the bird, dredge it, brown it, drench it, and simmer it tender. The usual additive for this process is, you guessed it, canned cream of mushroom soup. The first time this was done, I am pretty sure there were Lutherans in the room. Now, I do not disparage this formula, but it does sort of reduce things to the least common denominator. Surely we can make it more interesting.

In the first place, consider the breast and the balance of the bird as two distinct opportunities. For the breast, a couple of different fricassees are proven winners. The first option uses white wine. You filet off the pheasant breasts, setting the rest of the carcass aside. Season the breasts with salt and pepper and herbs — a mix like

Herbs de Provence works nicely — dredge them in flour, and brown them in some oil, along with some onion or maybe shallots. Drop in some mushrooms if you like. Add some white wine, and let the skillet simmer for a half hour or so. Serve over rice. Simple.

The other option uses jelly or syrup, resulting in a sweet sauce. Do everything as above, but instead of wine, add a couple of big dollops of an appropriate jelly, maybe sandhill plum; usually I use red currant jelly or syrup. Splash in a little dry sherry, too. This sauce is better over couscous than over rice. Now I know some of you guys from Pheasants Forever are rolling your eyes about that, but it is way better than anything you ever got out of your crockpot.

Now, what to do with the carcass? Boil it. Make a good broth, including some onions, some herbs, maybe some vegetable bouillon. Take the carcass out and strip the meat from the bones. After that you can go several ways.

Pheasant and dumplings is one good way to go. Easy, too — just add some frozen mixed vegetables, season to taste, thicken, drop in dumplings. Make a big pot, invite some people over. Pheasant noodle soup is fine, too. Both these offerings are distinctly pheasant, the broth deeper than chicken broth.

Recently we were out to a German-Hungarian dinner and got to talking with folks about what they called Pheasant Bubbagosh — that is what it sounded like they were saying. I finally figured out this was Paprikash, that is, a pheasant stew with lots of paprika. That is great, too.

Here, finally, is one more option for pheasant breast meat: green chile stew. Brown some bacon, then braise some dredged pheasant chunks in the bacon fat with some onion. Cook this into a stew with posole (hominy), chili powder, cumin, and of course, plenty of green chiles (we used the ones we dried last summer). Take a nap after dinner, because this lies like a bag of rocks in your stomach.

Darn it, now I am out of pheasants, and it is a long time until the stubble fields of autumn.

>·+·◆>··O··◆+·◄

You can tell by now that winter is a time when, deprived of the intensely sensate experiences of summer and fall, we try to make up for it with cooking, eating, and drinking. Never far from my mind, though, is what I sometimes refer to as the regional project — reflection on the characteristic stuff of life on the plains, and devisement of ways and means of living well here.

If there is to be a Great Plains cuisine, a style of cookery identifiable with the region, then surely it will arise from two elements. The first of these is ingredients from this place — good things that thrive here. The second is traditions from this place — traditions grounded in families, communities, and ethnic identities. So here goes with a couple of contributions to a Great Plains cuisine from our winter soup pot.

To begin with, we have been making a turkey noodle soup that seems to be well received wherever it goes as comfort food with a kick. We get our smoked turkey from the Hutterite colony; the point is, smoked turkey of identifiable origin and consistent quality. We are going for depth of flavor in the soup, so using smoked meat is a good start. Then we bolster the broth with chopped onion, diced carrot, vegetable bouillon, lots of dried lovage, dried parsley, garlic salt, and some marjoram.

For our noodles, no mechanical noodle maker is involved; these are hunky hand-made ones like my mother taught me — just egg, flour, and a little salt. Except we also roll cracked black pepper into them, quite a bit of it.

The big breakthrough came because we always have a jar of our dried green chiles from the garden sitting on the counter by the stove. We crumble these into the broth until we can taste the heat. Since these chiles are not terribly hot, they bring more depth than burn to the mix.

Serve with warm buttered bread, pickled beets alongside, and winter seems tolerable.

➤┈◆┈○┈◆┈◀

Venison has returned as a staple of Great Plains cuisine only in the past half-century, the first wave of pioneer settlement having pretty well eradicated deer from the prairies. The quality of venison cookery today, though, is distinctly uneven. Venison, being so lean, is an unforgiving meat. Moreover, its taste, so often spoken of with disdain as "wild" or "gamey," requires cooks to recognize that this is a different sort of red meat and to exploit its characteristics accordingly.

How often do you hear people say venison is the best meat for chili? Venison does make great chili, but to make the most of it, you need to align the seasonings with the flavor of the venison.

As you begin to brown the venison in the pot, you will need oil, because the venison is dry. Then, plenty of garlic. Sweet onion is fine to start out with the meat, but after that, garlic, and right in there with the browning meat, the herbs. Do not be shy with the chili powder and cumin. You also need plenty of bitter herbs — thyme, marjoram, and oregano, preferably some Mexican (or Greek) oregano. Put in some basil, too, for the tomatoes to come.

Canned diced tomatoes are fine, plus some tomato paste to thicken. For more liquid, add some canned enchilada sauce. For more complexity, add some mole paste.

At this point comes the most important element in aligning with the flavor of venison: adding red wine, and the right sort of red wine. It should be a red with plenty of tannins, and not subtle ones, either. My choice is Malbec. When you taste the product, there should be a great array of flavors rolling around in there, but foremost you have the alignment of the bitter venison, the garlic, and the Malbec tannins.

Pretty soon you will feel spring coming on, starting in your stomach.

On these northern plains, light is so important in our kitchens. We go to work in the dark, we come home in the dark, and we need for our kitchens to glow. The scents of favorite foods draw us in, we bathe in the light, and the owliness of winter is dispelled.

Our kitchens, too, can help to remind us of the virtues of continentality, that is, the joys of a four-season climate. In our house, the cuisine of early winter remains dominated by the prairie autumn.

Root crops figure prominently, with rutabagas holding the place of honor. Into every potato mash go cloves of garlic and a rutabaga, then a dollop of homegrown horseradish, plus sour cream and butter, resulting in a sensual mash so aromatic, so captivating and creamy yellow that the most ardent Adkins dieter is seduced.

Up from the basement, too, comes the crock of kraut, ready to stuff mallards, smother pork ribs, or wed to wurst on a traditional German plate. Be bold — embrace caraway and lard and peppercorns, and cook the stuff for a long, long time. Haralson apples sliced into every batch restore in the mind's eye the colors, along with the tastes, of autumn.

Likewise, the birds of autumn bring to the winter table recollections of comradeship, exertion, and the open land. Ringnecks, greenheads, honkers, sharptails, and if you are lucky, dainty Hungarian partridge.

The last of the cabbage of autumn, looking a little dark and curly in December, goes into a great batch of *Bierocks*, those wonderfully portable bundles of meat (I like pork in mine) and onions and cabbage wrapped in dough. I like to lift the towel from a batch of *Vorteig*, or batter-dough, and inhale the yeast.

Now comes deep winter, and with it new cravings. There dawns a frigid morning when it just seems right to cook Cream of Wheat. I know, this sounds like somebody's grandparents, but put some butter in it, sprinkle it with cinnamon, then add a big dollop of homemade applesauce, and see if that does not seem like eating dessert for breakfast.

Then nothing helps so much to make a winter morning seem surmountable as to have scrapple ready to fry. It is easy — fried ground pork and onions, seasonings, and cornmeal mush left to set in the fat, sliced into the skillet.

Darkest winter, when those surly lows settle in, calls for extreme measures. It is time to break out the chokecherry cordial. A handy student of mine named Dave Hammes taught us to grind our chokecherries so as to release rich almond and vanilla flavors into our jellies and syrups. That raised the question, what to do with all the chokecherry pulp that remained? Into a crock it went, along with a mound of sugar and a gallon of Everclear, to age a few months.

Now we decant, and in the bright kitchen, the purple product is luminous. After the first swallow, we rename the beverage. This is not chokecherry cordial. This is chokecherry hostile. It has attitude. It is a purple mule in a bottle. It is working. Winter, bring it on. Fetch me my skis and skates. I am fortified.

⊢·✦·○·◆·⊣

Years ago, when I was new to the northern plains, I had business with the priest of a small-town parish in south-central North Dakota. We talked through the matters before us, and it got to be about ten in the morning as we sipped coffee. At which point the good father, having concluded I was harmless, leaned over the coffee table and said, "Have you ever tried any of our red-eye?" And we did.

I am not advocating drinking here, I am talking about culture. Red-eye is a traditional, sweet, anise-flavored drink of the Black Sea Germans (and other eastern Europeans, it seems) of the northern plains. The main use for red-eye was as a *Hochzeit* (wedding celebration) drink. Commonly a couple of fellows would be stationed at the entrance to the hall. Adult male celebrants would not be allowed to enter until they had taken shots of the stuff.

The bottle of red-eye on my desk at home was mixed up according to a recipe given me by a distinguished academic administrator — well, I might as well say it was Jim Ozbun, former president of North Dakota State University — who got it from one of his West River buddies, a guy named Bill Jablonski. It goes like this.

First you burn (caramelize) two cups of sugar in a big, heavy skillet or pot. To this you add four cups of water, dissolving the caramel. (You'll have to stir and crush it; I use a wooden spoon.) Then add two more cups of sugar, nine more cups of water, and bring it all to a boil. Let the mixture cool, and pour in a liter of Everclear. Throw in a handful of stars of anise.

I let the red-eye season in a crock for a month or so before drawing it off into bottles; otherwise it tastes too much like rubbing alcohol. The color of the finished drink is reddish brown. It is heavily sweet. Some people drip in a little of the juice of maraschino cherries to redden the fluid up, but I am not that ecumenical. Some young folks these days dislike red-eye because it tastes of anise. Nordic Europeans who themselves put a bottle of aquavit into a snowbank for special occasions, though, will understand the appeal.

Now here is a serendipitous piece of good fortune that helps to take the edge off a hard winter. Having spent a good deal of time in Australasia, I have developed a taste for tea, especially on bitter days, drunk with sugar and milk. One winter night I was sitting down with a pot of tea by the fireplace, and there was the bottle of red-eye on my desk, and you can guess what happened. Great inventions often are spontaneous.

We need more signature items of regional taste, and it is important that this new drink acquire a good name, but I have not come up with one. It is about the color of the Little Missouri in spring rise. It is wonderfully warming when you come in with your skis or skates, and gentle on the palate, the anise complementing the tea perfectly. It makes you nod off in front of the fire with a feeling of well-being.

⊳┤⊕⊷○⊶┤⊲

This may be how a great regional cuisine comes into being. There are good things available, products of the place that are brought together by the admixture of lucky chance and cultural invention. Pay attention now, because this is good.

It all started with a bison roast, a big one, from a beast killed in a pasture and hung in a barn. Since the roast was large for my household, I trimmed off a pile of stew meat for separate use. The roast then went into a marinade — plum juice extracted from *Prunus americana*, the native plum of the northern plains, picked along the Sheyenne River.

Meanwhile the trim went into a kettle along with some onion, carrot, and herbs (a selection, mainly thyme and marjoram). Some garlic salt and vegetable bouillon deepened the broth. Then came the addition where the native met the Nordic: a diced rutabaga.

I had better add a word on behalf of the rutabaga, which English folk are inclined to call a Swede and feed to cattle. It is great winter provender, healthy, keeps forever if waxed, and adds both texture and taste to all sorts of cold-weather dishes.

As we tucked into the bison rutabaga soup — eating it with a dollop of sour cream, like borscht — I was unaware that it was National Rutabaga Month, as declared by the Advanced Rutabaga Studies Institute (everybody thinks I make this stuff up) in Forest Grove, Oregon. Forest Grove has been the self-declared Rutabaga Capital of the World since 1951.

Getting back to the main event, the bison roast, next day it went into a roasting pan along with some onions and carrots. I slipped whole cloves of garlic into little cuts in the top of the roast, rubbed it with ground pepper and coriander, then set it to bake at

325°F (bison meat roasts best at low temperature, because it is dense and conducts heat readily).

By the time the roast was done, it had given back much of the marinade as juice in the pan, which was the basis for a lovely gravy. The gravy, gently sour from the plum juice, was reminiscent of a *Sauerbraten*, only more delicate. The marriage of bison and plum juice is one made in heaven, or else in North Dakota.

Speaking of culinary unions, along with the roast and gravy we served a potato rutabaga mash, which we call potatobagas. Too bad we ate up all the mash, because potatobagas mixed with a little egg and flour and fried in butter make a great side dish for breakfast.

We are not done yet. There was leftover gravy. It happened, too, that I had just come home from an extension gig in Towner, North Dakota, bearing curds. I mean to say, I stopped in at Winger Cheese and loaded up. Most of the curds we already had eaten up beer-battered and fried, but the remainder there in the kitchen, along with the gravy, and a bag of Norkotah potatoes that were showing their age since I dug them the previous September, led to an obvious conclusion: poutine.

Well, it is obvious if you have spent time in Quebec, where poutine is the ultimate comfort food. Poutine is a plate of French fries covered with cheese curds and then slathered with brown gravy. Popular writers credit its invention to a restaurateur named Fernand Lachance in Warwick, Quebec, in 1957. He named it.

I figured that use of original ingredients gave me naming rights to the new regional concoction, which I dubbed Poutine Bison. It is a wonderful name, if you let yourself imagine the ways it might be spoken. Mutter it with Gallic diffidence from the corner of your mouth, or exclaim it with foppish glee, or growl it sensually from the back of your throat, punctuated with a guttural chuckle—Poutine Bison, heh-heh.

All right, I will stop playing with my food now.

I will bet many of you are like us. You go to your plant supplier and prowl the greenhouses way before it is time to buy and plant seedlings, just because the winter has been so long, and you need to be around green, growing things. Finally comes the day when you figure you can put things in the ground, and on account of pent-up desire, you drain your checking account.

We were going through the checkout with our seedlings at Neil Holland's Sheyenne Gardens when we spotted the yellow poster: Grandin Fire Department, Smelt Fry. It was right there next to Neil's poster explaining his Norwegian pricing system (round numbers, keep it simple).

So on the posted day in late May, we drive into Grandin. Lilacs are in bloom, peonies in bud. My companion asks, in all seriousness, how we will find the fire hall. In a town with only two retail businesses — a service station on one side of the interstate interchange, a bar on the other — I do not think finding our destination is going to be a problem. There it is — a brick engine barn with metal addition, right across the street west of the Land O'Lakes elevator. People are lined up out onto the sidewalk.

Inside, the sign at the ticket table informs us the tariff is $7.00 — darn, we could have saved a dollar by ticketing in advance. It turns out the price is cheap for what is offered.

By which I mean, first, this is a great feed. Serve yourself in the buffet line, piling on fried smelt as you wish, slaw, chips, buns, coffee. These smelt are the little ones, crisp, battered with a mixture of pancake mix and beer, deep-fried in canola oil. In the opposite corner there is a keg assiduously tended by a couple of firemen. The volunteer fire department counts about thirty on its roster, but there are about forty people working on this dinner, counting spouses and friends, all of them wearing red fire department T-shirts.

"This is a historic event," says Betsy Tate, taking a break from mixing batter, but inquiry among the volunteers cannot establish just how historic. They agree the smelt fry has been going on for thirty years at least, likely more. The current ramrod of the operation is Louis Rosenau, who buys the smelt from a supplier in Duluth — about 275 pounds of them. Tonight he prowls among the workers and customers, supervising and chatting. There is a lot of chatting going on. More than five hundred people will be served this evening.

It looks to me like the lowest job in the food chain is cleaning smelt. They come headless, but there are five or six people wearing latex gloves gutting the little morsels, a tedious job. A couple more people are battering them, and two to four are working the fryers. One or two of these guys are dipping snuff, and so for a while, I keep a special eye on them.

Aside from the main serving line is another station dispensing, the sign says, "Jack and Becky's Beans." Becky Indvik attends the roaster. For many years Jack "Porky" Rosenau handled the bean operation, but he got weary, and so the past four or five years Becky has been helping out.

Helping out seems to be a way of life with this crew. Any local emergency or need that comes up, there is likely to be some sort of benefit involving food at the fire hall. They have other regular events, too — a ham dinner on Palm Sunday, a steak fry in November. "It's a catering company disguised as a fire department," Betsy Tate quips from the fire hall kitchen threshold.

A country town has to find its center somewhere. Tonight, as on many nights, it is at the Grandin fire hall.

<hr />

If there were to be a North Dakota cuisine, what would it be? Now, some of you think I am setting up a punch line here, but I am not. My Suzzanne and I were invited to give a talk at the Ellendale Opera

House, and we gave out the title, "Range Management 101: The Idea of a Prairie Cuisine."

When we were asked to do this, it forced us to consider more seriously what we think about food and life on the plains, specifically North Dakota. In the first place, we cook a lot, and we eat a lot, too, or at least I do. We are omnivores. We eat junk, and we eat fine foods, and we enjoy life on the margins between the two. Most of all, we like to eat things that are somehow grounded in our lives. Things we raise or catch or gather or know the producers of, or things that hearken back to our roots.

So, getting back to the original question, what would a North Dakota cuisine look like? Here is what we think: three elements.

First, dynamic ethnic traditions. We have a rich array of historic traditions, most of them female-centered (with some specific male roles, like butchering), for putting food on the table. Some of these have fossilized. Lutefisk, for instance, is not really a food anymore; it is a sacrament, an homage. Knoephle are food. In living ethnic food traditions, people are still eating the stuff and working with it. There is ongoing improvisation and customization.

Second, distinctively regional materials. Good cookery often happens from having an embarrassing surplus of something around and asking, what can we do with this stuff? If, for instance, you are a good shot and have a good retrieving dog, you become inventive and expert in the preparation of pheasant for the table. Likewise, I am sure North Dakotans score higher than the national average for consumption of rhubarb. If we are going to eat the stuff, we should do it well.

Third—and this is the one most difficult to pin down — a culture of culinary aspiration. We have to want to have good food, food that brings people to the table, food that is a reason to talk to one another, food that is admired as it is consumed. One heartening thing is that young people across the country, including many of my own acquaintance, get this. More and more young people can cook, and they take an interest in it.

These three essential elements are related to, but not limited to, many of the trendy ideas in the air today — sustainability, locavorism, the slow food movement, the foodie movement. Talking about these ideas, we decided we are not snooty foodies. Nor are our inclinations toward cookery simply matters of sensuous delight, although we embrace that.

No, it comes around to the idea of food as identity. We are the kind of people who like a pot of great northern beans because they are great, because they are northern, and because our neighbors are combining them. We are the kind of people who like scrapple because our parents made it, and their parents made it; the kind of people who argue about the right way to make it, and we call that a mixed marriage.

It would be a good idea to have more arguments about food, and I do not mean about food pyramids and school lunches, I mean about food. Because we are what we cook.

⊱─◈─◇─◈─⊰

Y ou have to admire those Litchville ladies who back in 1992 cooked up *Ritzy Rhubarb Secrets*. Whereas other clubs and committees commonly produce cookbooks of local interest, they, without benefit of focus groups or advertising agencies, manufactured a cult classic.

Ritzy Rhubarb Secrets was published by the Litchville Committee 2000 and edited by Jane Winge. There are historical and technical sections, but the bulk of the book is devoted to recipes sorted by genre — Bars & Cookies; Beverages; Breads, Sweet Rolls & Muffins; Cakes; Desserts; Pies, Tarts, Crusts & Meringues; Preserves and Preservation; Puddings, Sauces & Soups; Salads; and Toppings & Glazes.

This is classic Dakota territory cookery, beginning with a staple characteristic of the region; merging the regional with the ethnic, as with rhubarb Kuchen; embracing individual variation and creation (everyone has her own rhubarb crunch); and finally going over the top — into culinary domains where personally, I do not wish to go — as with that rhubarb-and-red-hot upside-down cake.

Ritzy Rhubarb Secrets is a great gift for visitors and newcomers to our part of the country. It has gone through at least three printings, with more to come, I hope.

Around our place we have sharpened the chains on our saws and attacked the rhubarb forest once again. We have our crunch, and our muffins, and we have devised some new-age creations that break out of the Lutheran tradition.

Syrup is the key. *Secrets* gives instructions for extracting rhubarb juice, which is a simple matter. It also suggests making a light syrup from the juice. We make a heavy syrup — equal parts juice and sugar — and go from there.

For one thing, this syrup is good on another old standard, bread pudding. Melt a little butter (of course) in a saucepan, add syrup, and then finish off the sauce with a splash of whiskey, or maybe black currant vodka. (You can tell your relatives that the alcohol cooks off, which is a lie, but it sometimes satisfies them.)

Speaking of whiskey, how about this for a summer cocktail: equal parts of rhubarb syrup and bourbon (or whatever is your standard brown drink) in crushed ice. Then, to give it a real Dakota flourish, go out to the nearest slough and sniff around for some native mint. Wild mint around here differs from the garden varieties in both form (it flowers all along the stalk instead of at the end) and in scent (smells like the slough to me). Bruise the mint leaves into the glass.

Now that I have started down this road of decadence, I am going all the way, to another beverage that offers the ultimate in rhubarb sensuality. I am talking about the Lena Margarita.

Secrets contains various recipes for punches and slushes using rhubarb juice or syrup. Most of them incorporate something that partakes more of pop culture than of folklore — frozen lemonade, Kool-Aid, that sort of thing. Let us get back to basics. If you want a rhubarb drink, then make it a rhubarb drink.

You have a blender? Fill it with ice. Add about a cup of heavy rhubarb syrup. Then about a half-cup of tequila. Buzz it into a froth. You are done. My advice is to leave out the salt on the glass, as for me, it seems to conflict with the rhubarb, but suit yourself on that.

Naming these things is half the fun. The melodious "Lena Margarita" seems perfect. If you are not Norwegian, though, you might prefer the alternate name, "Tequila Borealis." Serve these to your guests unawares and they will be surprised, pleasantly.

>─┤◆>─○─<◆┤─<

They are not big pieces, but if you eat thirteen samples of Kuchen, that is about enough for an afternoon snack.

We arrived early for the Saturday session of the 87th Annual Tri-County Fair at the fairgrounds near Wishek, because we did not want to miss out on the 11th Annual Kuchen Contest, sponsored by BEK Communication (the communications cooperative of central North Dakota). The BEK ladies were setting out the entries in the stipulated categories: cheese, peach, rhubarb, apple, prune, wedding, and other. They asked, would you like to judge the Kuchen contest? Well, yeah!

Of course, you never want to judge Kuchen on an empty stomach, so we headed over to the concession stand and I had a Tonner burger: ton of hamburger, ton of cheese, ton of bacon, ton of pickles, ton of onions, and at least a ton of grease.

Then I tasted and evaluated entries in the rhubarb and wedding categories, according to a three-part rubric: taste, texture, and appearance. Really, they were all quite good. I have no idea who won, because by then, we were on to other things.

There were heifers being judged, pigs being shown, the kid calf contest, the tractor pull — which is more fun to be in than to watch — and all the other exhibits. There is also the carnival, which is not extensive, but it was interesting. It is hard to get a carnival contractor for a country fair, and so the fair board here bought its own suite of rides, fitted up its own booths, and runs the whole shebang with volunteers in red T-shirts.

After eating up the Tri-County Fair, we waddled back to the truck and put the pedal down for Ellendale, because you know, at 5:00 p.m. the Dickey County Fair serves a free pork dinner, with volunteers on their feet for hours filling plates until time for the rodeo. The pork dinner was interrupted by the final heat of the pig races, a coincidence not without irony. We saw good friends at the Dickey County Fair, but were not yet satisfied.

You see, on the way out we had stopped at Maple Valley Meats in Mapleton, because I like their Polish sausages, and then, when you get into a place like that, one thing leads to another, and pretty soon your cooler is too small. On the bulletin board was a poster promoting the American Legion baseball tournament in progress. So we decided to swing back for the night game after our fair circuit.

Which we did, and I tell you, Hendrickson Field, a community showpiece, was just spectacular under the lights, a field of dreams, the product of hard work and dedication. They tell me the baseball coach, Kevin Bratland, is also the groundskeeper, and he does a swell job. Not only was the field manicured, but the flower planters all around were flourishing, too.

The Enderlin team was not doing so well in the tournament, but Velva and Beulah played a close game, with Beulah staving off a late rally by Velva. I have to think the boys felt privileged to play in such a fine venue.

It had good hot dogs available, too, because this is, after all, the home of Maple Valley Meats. A good hot dog, some traditional ballpark snacks, and a starry drive home up the Kindred Road — it was a sweet Saturday, from Kuchen to CrackerJack.

➤⋅┼⋅◆➤⋅⋅○⋅⋅◆┼⋅◄

There are six old-fashioned cream cans, ten or eight or five gallons each, steaming atop propane burners, and a couple more packed and ready to cook — packed with layers of hearty vegetables and smoked sausage. The aroma drifting out of the hall, not to mention the gathering crowd, tells us we are just in time for the Sixth Annual Cream Can Supper in Dunn Center, North Dakota.

The supper is a fund-raiser for the Dunn County Historical Society and Museum. The idea is pretty simple. The cooking vessels are cream cans picked up at sales. Into the bottom of a can you stack, in this order, spuds, carrots, onions, cabbage, sweet corn, and sausage, in this case Cloverdale smoked Polish links. The can is filled about to the handles. Add some water, steam on a propane burner for an hour or so, and serve — by dumping the whole mess into the double wash tub that does duty as serving tray, or we might say, trough.

Add some bars (the zucchini bars were terrific, by the way), buns, and beverages, and you have a full meal deal. As is typical of outdoor feeds in this part of the country, the women do the organizing and the men do the cooking. Kory Richardson, the guy in the camouflage cap, seems to be in charge of the can crew.

Barb Fridley and Linda Kittelson provide some details about the operation. Last year they fed about 150 people, this year about 200. When they first started the event they cooked over coals in pits, but that was hazardous as well as laborious, and so Allen Lynch bought the propane burners.

The cooking takes place in a steel exhibit hall housing farm machinery, the serving in the parking lot. Inky Paulson and Marvin Sinnes, on fiddle and guitar, entertain the diners. Members of the Civil Air Patrol help with setup and supervise parking. It is a pretty efficient, relaxed operation.

The cause is good, because the Dunn County Historical Society is an all-volunteer operation, operating a museum with outstanding collections. Many of its artifacts are rare objects that speak from everyday life in the region. I doubt many people know what a calf blab is anymore, but they have one. Their ice plow, a device that mechanized the winter harvest of ice from local lakes, is a wonderful piece, as is their Woodman's Approved Prairie Fire Extinguisher, a chain-link drag for putting out prairie fires.

Hardly anyone in these parts has ever heard of a cream can supper, and in fact, the origins of the custom are a little murky. It is one of those things that sounds old-time authentic, but I cannot locate any documentation of it being done as a common or public event until recently. There is an outfit in Nebraska called the Ogallala Cream Can Supper Company that is marketing stainless steel cream cans, and it appears they have made up a mythology about feeding cowboys on the range in this fashion—which does not make a lot of sense to me, given the aversion of cowboys to milking, and to vegetables, likewise.

In recent years, though, cream can cooking, sometimes known as a "Polish luau," has spread across the country, its appeal being simplicity of preparation for large groups combined with a certain amount of hilarity around dumping the product into a trough of some kind and people tucking in with enthusiasm.

The music is done, the plates are cleared, but people linger at the tables to chat and enjoy the low light and evening air. We are on the cusp of autumn. Satisfaction is more than a matter of a full stomach.

8. BLOOMING IN RICHER COLOR

Wherein the prairie historian ponders Eric Sevareid's question:
What am I doing here?

"I may not know who I am," Wallace Stegner once wrote, "but I know where I am from." He knew how important it is to situate yourself. This is what he called "the sense of place."

Unfortunately, many people of the Great Plains are not so clear about the sense of place as was Stegner. Sharon Butala, who lived and wrote near Stegner's old home of Eastend, Saskatchewan, told me she wrote an essay to be included in a new book being published in Canada, and she referred to her home country as "the Great Plains." The publisher had the essay reviewed by an academic in Winnipeg who insisted she could not call her own country "the Great Plains," that the only appropriate term in Canada was "the Prairies."

This was odd, as it was Henry Kelsey, explorer for the Hudson Bay Company, who first called the grassy middle of North America "Great Plains" when he emerged from the northern forest in what is now Saskatchewan in 1690. I also checked the map in the classic travel narrative of the Canadian west, W. F. Butler's *Great Lone Land*, 1872, and right there in the middle of the Canadian Prairies it says, "Great Plains."

In the United States it is the term "Midwest" that causes confusion about the Great Plains. People think that "Midwest" is a term referring to something midway east and west, between the East and the West. In fact, as the geographer James Shortridge explains, the term "Middle West" arose to designate something between north and south. In the nineteenth century there was the Southwest, there was the Northwest (Montana, the Dakotas, and Minnesota), and then there was the Middle West — basically Kansas and Nebraska. In the twentieth century, though, the labels "Middle West" and "Midwest" expanded to the east and north.

Late in that century people in Michigan, Wisconsin, and Minnesota (particularly the last) coined the term "Upper Midwest" so as to distinguish themselves in this emerging middle region. Subsequently people in eastern North Dakota who sent their insurance premiums east to Lutheran Brotherhood, rooted for the Vikings, liked to shop in Minneapolis, and kept cabins in the Minnesota lake country also adopted the "Upper Midwest" label. The problem is that no part of North Dakota is midwestern. North Dakota is the most plains state of all — the most level, the least timbered, the most perfectly semiarid. So some namers of North Dakota began to speak of "the Upper Great Plains," which is to say, they are really mixed up.

Then folks in Montana got into the naming game by commencing to call eastern Montana "the High Plains." Perhaps they had seen too many Clint Eastwood movies. The High Plains are a distinct province of the plains stretching from West Texas through my old home in western Kansas up to Pine Ridge, South Dakota, and nowhere near Montana. Now there is even a newspaper published in Fargo, North Dakota, that calls itself the *High Plains Reader*. To people in Grand Forks, this may seem to go beyond geographic confusion and almost sound like a cruel joke. During the Big Water of 1997, they wished that they lived on some high plains!

Situate yourself, Stegner said. Work out a sense of place that is true to where you are. That is what I tried to do when I lived in Emporia, Kansas. I lived on the same street as had the great Progressive, and undoubtedly midwestern, editor, William Allen White, and within oppressive smelling range of the Bunge soybean processing plant. On the other hand, the other side of town smelled of beef, beef from the plains. I concluded that the boundary of the Great Plains ran right up Commercial Street, that Emporia was half midwestern and half Great Plains.

This taught me a lesson, so that when in 1992 I moved to my new position in Fargo, North Dakota, I looked for a house in West Fargo, home of the Packers. No more midwestern identity crises for me. As for your own sense of place — work it out for yourself. Except if you have not already noticed, I spend a lot of time trying to influence your thinking on the matter.

⊱┈✦┈◯┈✦┈⊰

Childhood on the prairies has a way of staying with you for the rest of your life. In the preface to her Nebraska novel, *My Antonia* — the greatest novel ever written about life on the Great Plains of North America in my opinion — Willa Cather speaks of the "freemasonry" of those who grew up on the plains. They know things they cannot explain to people who have not shared the same experiences.

One of Cather's greatest admirers was Stegner, who wrote about his boyhood in southwestern Saskatchewan in *Wolf Willow.* Stegner's book hinges on what is called a "sensory trigger" — that is, some impression of the senses that takes you back to a past time and place, makes you think about that time and place without really knowing why you are thinking about it.

Stegner goes walking along the Frenchman River in his old

hometown, and suddenly it comes upon him: "the smell that has always meant my childhood . . . that odor that I have not smelled since I was eleven, but have never forgotten. . . . It is wolf willow, now blooming with small yellow flowers. It is the wolf willow . . . that brings me home."

The smell of wolf willow is powerful, and musky. It is pleasant only if it connotes good memories. For people from other parts of the plains, it is similar to that of Russian olive in bloom, but not so sweet.

The memories loaded into the scent are what are important. Stegner gets this idea of a sensory trigger — smell triggering memory — from the French writer, Marcel Proust. Proust is famous for recalling the whole village where he spent his summers of boyhood from the scent of a teacake.

Stegner, being a 1950s writer, was much taken by pop psychology — nature and nurture, imprinting, all that sort of thing. So he was much taken with the psychological phenomenon of a sensory trigger described by Proust. All of which makes this discussion sound hopelessly literary and esoteric, except when you think about it, most of us with prairie personal histories can cite examples of a smell conjuring up past experiences. Alfalfa, fresh-mown, is a common one, recalling up the joys and the labors of hayfields past. For persons of a certain generation, Aqua Velva calls back certain male relatives, or Evening in Paris past female acquaintances.

For me, the scent of certain soil types does it. Although I live in North Dakota, I travel north and south frequently, and it is the soils of the Platte and particularly the Arkansas river valleys that smell like home to me as I roll down the truck window. For my wife — and this is a source of humor to anyone she tells it to — the sensory trigger is DEET. She grew up in Alaska, so every outdoor memory of her youth is permeated with insect repellant.

Which raises the question, what is your sensory trigger? What scent takes you home to another place and time?

I explained to one of my classes how the godfather of the memory trigger in literature, Proust, experiences memories rushing upon him when he consumes a morsel of madeleine — a cookie — dipped in tea. I cited to them the example of Stegner and the musky scent that brought him home on the Frenchman River. Then I asked them, what is your memory trigger? It was late in the term, a time of stress and homesickness. Predictably, quite a few responses referred to parents and family.

A quiet fellow remembered "the taste of rhubarb slush, made by my mother in the summer." A young woman recalled "the scent of Virginia Slim cigarettes and spearmint gum. I was an anxious child," she explains, "and my mother would always comfort me. She smoked Virginia Slims and chewed spearmint gum."

"Coffee and coffee cake," chimed in another respondent. "My mom had a bit of a tradition — Wednesday mornings in the wintertime, she would have a few neighbor ladies over to visit, and as a kid before I went to school, I would always sip watered down coffee with mom. She made it with cinnamon or nutmeg, and that mixture with a hint of coffee takes me back to those mornings." Then there was the fellow who blurted out, "Knipco heater. Working in the garage with my dad."

Well, this is enough to make those of you with kids in college eager to welcome them home for the holidays, I am sure, but where are the rough-and-ready recollections of the open prairies? We have those, too — the smell of freshly worked ground, the taste of Red River Valley clay clinging to fresh-dug carrots.

In the realm of outdoor memories I notice a distinct shift, having to do with gender, in recent years: young women are getting into farm work, field work, and it registers in their memories. One of them recalled "the smell of alfalfa dried just to where it is time to bale" — so I am pretty sure she was running the baler.

Another of these women thought of "the smell of moist dirt, green corn, and above all the smell of moisture in the air. In the summer when it was over 100 degrees and dry as a bone all day, I would be up at 4 a.m. in the cool moistness of the morning air that the parched corn seemed to gobble up. My old diesel Chevy got me to the field each morning where I would move water to irrigate the corn field. There was something about the eternal dryness that changed the way it smelled when there was finally some moisture in the air."

So now I am reassured about the next generation of farm operators on the prairies, but also sympathetic with the young man leaning his crutches on his desk. He is a varsity wrestler, out for the season, missing the competitive Big 12 schedule. What's your memory trigger, lad?

"Wrestling mat smell," he said.

The sense of place, as the basis of personal identity, is not just a matter of perception, but also of expression. The editor of the student newspaper and a photographer here at NDSU dropped by, said they were doing a story about me. When it came to the photo shoot, they said, get your hat—the broad-brimmed, tan, felt Akubra I wear most of the year. Evidently they regard it as some kind of signature.

Which I guess it is, since I most always wear either the Akubra or a black Stetson to work. What is the deal with that? Well, I do spend a lot of time in Australia or New Zealand, and folks in Australasia are really melanoma-conscious. That southern sun just stings. In Australia school kids are not allowed out for recess without a broad-brimmed hat. Remembering those deep sunburns I got on an open-platform 930 Case as a kid in western Kansas, I figure I ought to take precautions.

For me as a historian of grassy places, though, there is more meaning to the hat. In the back of the main lecture hall at the Australian National University, Canberra, is a photo portrait of the man for whom the hall is named, the great historian Manning Clark, wearing his battered old Akubra.

I had one that looked just like that until a few years ago, when our Labrador retriever, who had a remarkable vertical jump, snatched it from the top of the hat-rack one night and chewed it into nickel-size pieces. I still wonder what possessed him, and how many years he thought about doing that before he did it, presuming Labrador retrievers think. Now I am trying to break in a new hat properly.

Years ago when I had a cushy appointment as a research scholar at the Turnbull Library in New Zealand, the head librarian walked in to meet me and said, "The last chap in here with a hat like that was Manning Clark." I said, thank you.

Here is another picture of a professorial hat I like. The Western History Collections at the University of Oklahoma hold a photograph of a youthful Edward Everett Dale, OU's cowboy professor. There is Dale in a canvas shirt, the tail of his tie tucked into the front buttons, and of course, a tan Stetson atop his head. The wonderful thing is the photo was taken in a studio with a backdrop of painted palm trees.

Dale, though, was the kind of professor that I imagine, on parents' day, college kids would point out and say, "Looky there's Professor Dale." He taught Western American history, having studied at Harvard with Frederick Jackson Turner, but he never forgot his roots on the Oklahoma range, where he had cowboyed, among other jobs, and been a deputy sheriff. Dale was a legendary storyteller. I think it was pretty easy to get him off the subject.

In 1967 OU opened a new social science building, and they christened it Edward Everett Dale Hall. It is a plain, boxy high-rise, but anyway, they named a building after him.

I have learned things from these two guys with hats, Clark and Dale. Clark taught me that you have to treat all the people in the historical past with pity, if not love. I think he meant what today people would call empathy. Dale taught me, remember where you came from. You are still pretty much the same as these kids from Watford City or Peabody or Benkelman who turn up in your classes there at the university.

Maybe, I hope, the hat says that to them.

⊱┈✦┈◦┈✦┈⊰

The sod house is the single most compelling symbol of Euro-American pioneering on the plains. It evokes domesticity, democracy, and the land in one powerful package. The most monumental photographic images of sod houses are the Nebraska photographs of Solomon Butcher. The single most celebrated image of a sod house, however, comes from Walsh County, North Dakota, and its story is intriguing.

The photograph dates from the late 1890s, its location commonly given as Milton, North Dakota, which is a little confusing; actually the photographer, John McCarthy, was from Milton, in Cavalier County, whereas the house and the homestead on which it stood were in neighboring Walsh County. The home was that of John and Marget Bakken, Norwegian homesteaders, and their two children, Tilda and Eddie.

Sure enough, with the help of friends in NDSU Archives, I find properties with the name John Bakken in a 1910 atlas of Walsh County. The homestead eighty acres is in S14 T158N R58W, which is to say, Silvesta Township. The house was in the NE/4 of the NE/4. Bakken also acquired the other eighty acres in the quarter, as well as another eighty acres in an adjoining section.

According to a family history and a published Walsh County history, John Bakken was born in Benson, Minnesota, in 1871. His parents were from Telemark, Norway. After a sojourn in Minnesota, they moved their large family to homestead in North Dakota in 1881. There John married Marget Axvig, who also came from a big

Norwegian settler family, she having been born in Telemark in 1867.

John and Marget took their own homestead and were pioneers of mythic cast. During the starving time early in their marriage Marget fed the household on bread, syrup, and lard, supplemented with milk from the cows she milked. John made the furniture and the straw mattresses. When snow drifted over the soddy, he shovel-carved thirteen steps from the door to the sunlit surface. They built a good frame barn in 1904, while still living in the sod house, and finally moved into a frame house of their own in 1906.

It was in 1898 that McCarthy photographed the family in front of their house. The low, rounded roof is overgrown with weeds and grass and punctuated with stovepipes. The situation of the family members perfectly represents traditional gender and age roles. Marget stands at the door, a washbasin in hand. John stands off to the left, spade in hand. Tilda and Eddie, both in dresses as was common at the time, stand on ground well out from the house, children of the country. The family dog is a blur under the window.

You can view the photo at the American Memory website of the Library of Congress, part of the Fred Hulstrand collection posted there by the Institute for Regional Studies. Hulstrand was a photographer who bought out McCarthy in Milton and operated his own studio in Park River. His assistants, the Wick sisters, Thelma and Sylvia, colorized photographs with oil paints. The exhibited photo is one of their colorized prints.

The fame of the photo came about when an artist from the United States Treasury Department noticed it in a book called *Pageant of America*. His reproduction of the image became the Homestead Act centennial stamp, four cents, issued in 1962. The stamp shows subtle changes in the composition of the image, and one glaring change — the removal of the children (allegedly to avoid depiction of living persons). The dog is gone from the image, too. On issuance of the stamp, however, John Bakken, still living in North Dakota, recognized himself and his old soddie.

Another artist's adaptation of the same photo appeared on the "Utvandringen til Amerika" postage stamp issued in 1975 by Norway to commemorate immigration to America. This one restores the children to their rightful place. Indeed, the postures of John and Marget make the children central to this postal image—rightly so, given the attitudes of immigrant settlers. In this Norwegian stamp image, the dog is back, too.

My students believe I am a living antiquity, because I went to a one-room country school and remember our ring from the party line (three longs and two shorts). For the sake of grounding, sometimes I wish there was a sod house in my lineage, but I will not cross the line and make one up.

▷─┼─◆▷─◇─◁▷─┼─◁

D riving to Fort Abercrombie with a van-load of students, I recalled one of them hailed from the nearby little town of Christine. I asked him if he knew how the town got its name. Here is the story.

Two stories exist, actually, with variations of same. Descendants of pioneer farmers Knute and Kristine Norby, who lived in a dugout at the site, say the town was named for Mrs. Norby. The founders thought about naming it Knute, but Christine was more felicitous.

The predominant opinion, however, is that the town was named for the Swedish operatic soprano, Christina Nilsson, although oral traditions along these lines diverge. One says that as the famous singer passed through town on the Milwaukee Railroad, she waved from the train, and so the town was named for her. The problem with this story is that the naming of the Christine post office in 1884 preceded the railroad by a couple of years.

The more straightforward story is that the town's founder, John Bisbee, was an admirer of the soprano, known as "the Swedish nightingale," and so named the town after her. This would have appealed to the ethnic sentiments of nearby settlers.

Likewise they would have identified with her remarkable life story. She was the daughter of farmers in Småland, and her family experienced the economic malaise and population pressures that were the drivers of Swedish emigration to North America. Her father, too, was a church choir leader, and Christina was a popular performer as a child, helping out the family fortunes by playing the violin and singing in inns and at fairs.

In about 1857, while singing at the summer fair in Ljungby, Christina was discovered by a patron, a magistrate who offered to pay for her musical training, first in Halmstad and Stockholm, then on to Paris. The young singer had a striking physical presence, accented by her amber hair and azure eyes, and patronage allowed her to develop her musical gifts.

Following her operatic debut as Violetta in Verdi's *La Traviata*, Christina Nilsson rapidly achieved rampant celebrity. Her appearances in Paris, London, and across Europe were sensational. American fans, especially Swedish-American fans, clamored for an American tour. Nilsson made a two-year performance tour across America in the early 1870s, after which she went to London to marry a wealthy French financier in Westminster Abbey. Thereafter she mixed freely with European royals and capitalists, while her singing career waxed even more triumphal. Her voice was not powerful, but it was sweetly lyric, captivating.

In 1882–83 Nilsson made her third North American performing tour; in the latter year a general store marked the site of Christine, Dakota Territory; and the following year the post office of Christine was established in the store. Thus the correspondence of Nilsson's tour with the surge in Swedish and Scandinavian immigration to the United States, and with the founding of Christine, argues for the veracity of the operatic theory of name origin for this little country town.

Here is the cool part of that. Christina Nilsson was the prototype for the character of Christine in the 1910 novel by Gaston Leroux, *The Phantom of the Opera*. This led to the creepy 1925 silent film by the same name. Which led to the 1986 musical by Andrew Lloyd Webber and stardom for Sarah Brightman.

So what does Christine, North Dakota, present population about 150, get from all this? Just the story, and a little afterglow of celebrity.

⊱•⊰•◦•⊰•⊱

There were regrets in the wake of disaster, as people in western North Dakota considered the circumstances and consequences of the Rocky Ridge School fire of November 6, 1914. The fellows working on Melvin Greenwood's threshing outfit regretted moving the rig across country near Fryburg on a dry, windy day, so that sparks from the steam engine, lighting in the dry grass, sprang up as fierce flames out of control.

Twenty-one-year-old schoolteacher Gladys Hollister, as she lay dying of extreme burns, regretted having told the schoolchildren to flee the fire, rather than just hunkering down in the one-room schoolhouse, which in the end came through the fire unscathed. Six children, along with the teacher, paid the ultimate price for that decision.

Miss Hollister and her thirteen students gazed with alarm out the school windows as the towering prairie fire swept toward Rocky Ridge School, generally called the Davis school, near Belfield. She instructed the students to make a break for a nearby plowed field. Three of them made the run safely. Others got caught by the fire but came through all right onto bare ground. Miss Hollister and Ruth Olson, a twelve-year-old girl, also made the plowed field, but then they noticed a group of five boys who were going the wrong way. The teacher and Ruth went after them, and were overcome, with them, by the flames.

The first persons on the scene after the fire were two farmers, Frank Davis and William Pike, who lost a son in the blaze. Three victims were dead; the others lived for a while, and they talked about what had happened. Miss Hollister, carried to the schoolhouse, died there. She would be carried back home for burial in Mapleton, Iowa.

The six children who perished in the fire all were buried in Belfield, following funeral observances that released a deluge of grief. The little white caskets were placed in a row in the Belfield opera house. Floral tributes were profuse, one of them bearing a large placard reading, "Memoir of Our Dear Teacher." Three pastors — Norwegian Lutheran, German Lutheran, and Presbyterian — officiated. Twenty-four Belfield schoolchildren served as pallbearers. Some seven hundred mourners turned out for the services, but only half could get into the building. The funeral cortege was three-quarters of a mile long.

The editor of the *Belfield Times* exercised his full rhetorical powers in a lengthy expression of community grief.

> Never before has it fallen our lot to record a funeral
> where life ended with such a sorrowful and heart-
> rending history as the one held in the opera house
> Tuesday afternoon over the six little corpses who so
> tragically and untimely passed to the soothing arms
> of their Maker last Friday, helpless victims, with their
> teacher, of the prairie fire which swept across a large
> stretch of country southwest of town. Words fail us in
> our effort to express the dark gloom which fell over the
> city, or the horror stricken faces of our citizens.

Of heroic young Ruth Olson, who tried to save her brother, the editor wrote in remembrance, "We cannot think of Ruth as dead, but, as a flower wafted to a distant shore, touched by a Divine hand, blooming in richer color and sweeter fragrance than those of earth."

In her book on the history of prairie fire, historian Julie Courtwright writes of the tendency of prairie folk to erect memorials to fire victims after the fact, especially during the 1930s. This never happened with the Davis school fire. Perhaps that should be redressed. A century later, it should be possible to make a respectful site of remembrance without opening old wounds. This site of tragedy and courage should be marked.

▻⊶⊶○⊷⊶◅

The eradication of wild buffalo from the Great Plains was symbolic of something larger: the killing off of most all large wild animals that happened with settlement of the prairies by farmers and ranchers. The large herbivores were killed off for eating; the large predators were killed off because they were incompatible with livestock husbandry.

Now today, with the emptying out of the rural landscape, and the resurgence of deer populations, we observe the gradual return of predators to the plains. People on the plains love to tell mountain lion stories. Gray wolves, too, are beginning to appear again in coffee-klatch story sessions. It seems to me only a matter of time before grizzlies emerge from their mountain fastnesses to reoccupy their old range on the plains. That will be interesting.

Not yet forgotten are legendary encounters with outlaw wolves on the plains a century ago. Families pass these stories down and record them in local histories. The greatest of all the outlaw wolves was Old Three Toes. The name is significant to the legend. It seems that Three Toes was exceedingly wary, and thus became Old Three Toes, because as a youngster he had lost a toe in a trap. He had suffered contact with humankind, and was embittered by it. His depredations appear in legend not as mere grocery shopping by an ordinary predator but as the vendetta of a vengeful renegade.

The best telling of the legend of Old Three Toes appears in the shepherd memoir, *Sheep*, by Archer B. Gilfillan. Gilfillan was a college graduate who chose the profession of sheepherding from the 1910s to the 1930s. Three Toes depredated livestock in western

South Dakota from 1913 to 1925. Popular estimates of the value of stock killed ran to $50,000. Three Toes was reported to have killed twenty cattle in one night and sixty-five sheep in two nights.

According to Gilfillan, Three Toes eluded all pursuers for more than a decade. One fellow ran the wolf across fresh snow for ninety-five miles, changing horses five times, but was unable to close on him. Another pair of hunters chased the wolf forty miles from the Cave Hills to the Short Pine Hills, changing horses as they went, only to have the wolf double back on them to their own ranch in the Cave Hills! When tracked by dogs, Three Toes leaped across chasms and down embankments.

Then in 1925 Clyde F. Briggs, a predator control specialist imported from New Mexico, arrived in Harding County on a mission to take down Three Toes. He set his traps patiently along every likely line of travel, flanking every wolf set with extra traps to take out coyotes and leave the wolf set intact. This guy Briggs was resolute. If they ever make a movie out of this story, I think Briggs should be played by Tommy Lee Jones.

On July 23, 1925, Briggs found Three Toes in one of his traps. He tried to bring in the old beast, six feet long and only seventy-five or eighty pounds, alive, but Three Toes died in transport. Briggs, a salaried state employee, refused any monetary reward for the capture of Three Toes, but local ranchers took up a collection and presented him with a watch.

Sometimes I think it is a wonder that we of the settler society ever managed to develop any constructive sense of place in this land. We arrived with an old country longing, what the Swedes like those of Christine called *hemlängtan*, a homesickness that went away only with the passing of the immigrant generation. Both Atlantic immigration and prairie settlement were full of trauma, peril, and tragedy. We tell stories like that of the Rocky Ridge school fire not because they are unique but because they are representative. Settling in here on the plains, we did battle with nature and its creatures. The only positive side to the battle is that we feel nostalgia, a type of regret, over the fate of such resistance figures as Old Three Toes.

The naturalization to the land begins in the first native-born generation, but it takes time, and it remains a work in progress.

⊱―◈―〇―◈―⊰

"Up in very north North Dakota," the story goes, "near Walhalla or LeRoy, there is a grassy path known as White Lady's Lane. It is a grassy, weedy, un-kept-up dirt road off a gravel road.

"As you drive down the road you come upon a bridge over a small creek. If you drive there at night, as many teenagers like to test out, you can see a woman hanging from the bridge in a wedding dress."

The students in my classes at NDSU, bless their hearts, tell me stories. Every year comes a new harvest of legends of the plains.

The prologue to the White Lady legend is that the young woman had been party to a shotgun wedding, religious parents compelling the couple to marry shortly after a child was born. The day of the wedding, the bride checked the crib and found the baby dead. She then hanged herself from the bridge in her wedding dress.

"Many have seen the figure of the woman hanging there," my informant says. "Some will say that it is the woman haunting, while others will say it is the lights of Walhalla off in the distance."

Quite a few of these stories are linked to legend trips, that is, night-time adventures of teenagers who go to scary places and hope something goes bump in the night. These legends are place-specific. "I'm from a small town in western North Dakota called Hazen," begins another one of them. "About 10 miles north of town there's the remnants of a town called Krem."

This legend-tripper recounts the excursion off the highway, up a series of gravel roads, past the old Krem cemetery, filled mainly with infant burials. After that you come to another cemetery, this one filled with iron crosses and a large wooden cross tipped over under a pine tree. Then beyond that is the old Krem townsite, now retaining only a small group of brick and rock houses.

The observant excursionist will notice, some fifty yards outside the second cemetery, a lone headstone with inscription in German and Latin. The story of that headstone came to my informant by way of a lady in the rest home.

The deceased was a preacher, we are told. "He was newly out of seminary school, and he was in his mid-20s. He carried on a successful church for a few years, but then a little girl turned up missing. . . . The preacher committed suicide rather than face the charges.

"Well, the story goes, if you drive through the circle of the old brick and rock houses three times, the man will appear and speak to you." That is a story with powerful elements of history in it. There are new ones emerging, though, just as surely as fieldstone surfaces every spring. North of Maddock, we are told by another writer, there is a house along Highway 30. A high school student named Bob lived there, and he noticed some strange things happening. A tall kid, his feet sometimes stuck out from the blankets at night, and they became freezing cold. When he awoke, his breath made steam in the frosty air — but when he got up, the room temperature was comfortable. His family eventually moved away to Texas, and the house stood vacant.

"One night this summer after the 4th of July," my narrator recounts, "a bunch of my friends went out there." Lights were on in the house, but when they entered, through a basement window, the lights cut out. "They went to the kitchen and all the cupboard doors were shut. All of a sudden they started opening and slamming shut."

The gang of adventurers fled to their cars, where they discovered that several of them had gashes on their bodies, although no tears in their clothing. "One of the girls called Bob in Texas and he told her that sort of stuff happened to him a lot. This is a true story, one of my best friends was out there and came back to town hysterical. To this day nine of them still have the exact same story." Which means it must be true.

>—+—◆>—◦—<◆—+—<

"I used to tramp through there when I was going to country school," says Hilton "Bud" Sollid. "These things leave an imprint. I remember all the buildings, the people."

He is talking about the town of Simcoe, North Dakota. Grandson of Norwegian homesteaders, Bud was born in 1920 and grew up on a farm about a mile southwest of Simcoe. The school was just north of town. He and his brothers walked up Main Street on the way to school, picking up town kids as they went. "We all walked in a bunch to school," he says.

No businesses operate in Simcoe today. Nearly all the buildings have been moved away, except the depot, which was torn down. The elevator opens seasonally to receive grain. There are services every other week in the Lutheran church. Lots of prairie towns have gap-toothed main streets. Simcoe's is just about toothless. Except in the mind, and the art, of Bud Sollid. Because of him, I have seen Simcoe the way he saw it as a schoolboy.

He lets me in the back door of the Sons of Norway hall (converted from a general store in 1918), which is cold but well-kept. The meeting room has a good hardwood floor. Wooden folding chairs line the walls. "We used to have some wing-ding dances here in the 1930s. Twice a month the place would be packed," Bud remembers.

Bud does remember. And on the stage at the end of the hall, the material expression of his memory is arranged on plywood atop sawhorses. He has built a model of the town as he recalls it from the 1920s and 1930s. The buildings are of 1/4" plywood. Their walls are painted with thick paint smeared in rows to look like horizontal siding. The roofs are shingled with little rectangles of sandpaper.

The model town is anchored by its two elevators — the Farmer's Elevator and the Osborn McMillan. The Equity Hall is just across the Great Northern tracks north of the Farmer's Elevator, and across Main, west of the hall, is the depot. Lined up north from the depot on the west side of Main are all the town's businesses, with the Sons of Norway pegging the north end. On the east side of Main is just a gas station. That side is low ground, with a slough adjoining. Catty-corner northeast from the Sons of Norway is the church, next to which is Bud's grandfather's blacksmith shop. Residences encircle the business area.

This is "memory art" — the term that has come to be applied to the work of folk artists who recreate the past as they experienced it, in documentary fashion. And the model town is not all. Bedecking the walls of the hall are scenes of Simcoe that Bud has painted, along with some scenes of Norway as he has imagined them.

Here is something interesting about the painting style. There is one painting of a farm scene that shows sophisticated technique in the form of a schooled realism. This is not memory art. The scenes from memory, on the other hand, all assume the sort of naive painting style that is characteristic of so many memory artists. People are stylized. Distance, scale, and proportion are simplified or discarded. It is to say, disciplined realism is inadequate to express memory truly.

This is beautiful work, powerful work, moving work. It tells us much more than photographs could. Photographs — even in the days of glass plates — could be dispassionate, clinical. They only register light. Paintings like these register heat and motion.

There, in that painting of the tall merry-go-round in the schoolyard, see those three boys in overalls at lower right? The one on the left end, that's Bud.

Outside again I ask him, What is that room-sized chamber of concrete in the vacant lot on the west side of Main? He says that is the bank vault, left there when the bank was torn down. Back in the 1920s that concrete vault foiled a bank robbery, as the robbers despaired of cracking it. The bank closed anyway in 1928.

▷⊶⊶○⊷⊰◁

The good people in the public relations office of my university sometimes get a little exasperated with me. They ring me up and say such-and-such an eastern newspaper, or such-and-such a metropolitan magazine, would like to interview me for some story it is doing about North Dakota. To which I reply, not interested.

This response is based on experience. The story already is written. Eastern reporters call to get snippets of local color to fit into a predestined scheme. Give them what they want, and you end up patched into some story you realize afterward you do not want to be identified with.

Which raises the whole issue, one I do not talk about much, of the image of North Dakota as expressed elsewhere. We seem to care about this a lot. I am going to try to explain why I do not care much about it.

Do you remember "The Emptied Prairie," that depressing article, and the even more depressing photographs, that appeared in *National Geographic* in 2008? Reviewing that piece today, it is easy to understand why the reaction hereabouts was so angry. "Ghost towns stud North Dakota," the author intones, underneath a photograph of an abandoned farmhouse and some desiccated bones, "and this empty house is just one bone in a giant skeleton of abandoned human desire."

Disregarding the overwrought prose and the artificial photographs, both of which are staples of *National Geographic*, there remains the characterization of North Dakota as a perverse wasteland. Nothing in the piece is specifically false; it is just grossly selective, offering no other way of viewing the place other than that of the visiting firemen who work for *National Geographic*. This emptied prairie of which you write, we already know it, repopulated by the adventurous stories of our youthful legend trippers, reconstituted by the memory models and childlike paintings of our elders. What do you think you can tell us about it?

Now comes the same magazine with a cover feature, "Bakken Shale Oil: The New Oil Landscape." A different author, but the same photographer, this time offering spectacular images of an industrializing prairie, peopled by skilled laborers who are, in the author's words, "almost heroic." Almost, but not quite, I guess.

The content of this new article is utterly predictable, describing a "fracking frenzy" providing energy for the nation and opportunity for individuals, but of course, "at what cost?" I am not ridiculing the question, I am just laughing at the idea anyone would turn to *National Geographic* for the answer to it.

Lengthen your memory, and consider "Tough Times on the Prairie," the magazine's characterization of North Dakota in 1987.

Neoclassical beauty in the emptied prairie: Gascoyne School

Tough times, for sure, and here are the people of the prairies, carrying on in Norman Rockwell fashion, apparently oblivious of what the omniscient author knows, that their way of life is doomed, doomed, doomed. Like the other articles, the voice of the 1987 piece is essentially colonialist. A land out of time.

How about we just get over this? How about, the next time some fly-by-night think tank in California or New Jersey sends out a press release saying North Dakota ranks first in efficiency of pencil sharpeners, or forty-seventh in kindness to bunny rabbits, we refrain from giving the distributors free publicity? Why should we care? Might we not consider the questions of our well-being for ourselves, and come up with our own answers?

Excessive interest in external validation signifies a lingering insecurity not befitting of North Dakota in the twenty-first century. How are things going? We can take a look around and decide for ourselves.

⊱──◦──⊰

North Dakota is going to hell in a handbasket. Or, it is finally coming into its own. Depends on who you ask. As if this were something new, or profound. Ours is a storied land, and the storytellers are fighting it out for the last word. As if there ever was a last word.

Twenty years ago the historian William Cronon, himself a great storyteller, told a story about stories on the Great Plains of North America. He began with the elephant in the middle of the room: the Dust Bowl, and the stories that have been told about it.

Consider first the tale as told by Paul Bonnifield, a railroad brakeman and cowboy and wild horse catcher with a PhD in History, in his book about the Dust Bowl. Paul likes his bourbon neat, and he loves his neighbors. For him, the story of the Dust Bowl is one of prairie people resilient, hanging on in the face of a terrible drought, and at the same time, fending off the aggressive actions of a federal government that undermined their efforts.

Consider next the story told by Donald Worster, a historian whose palate bears the academic imprint of that silver spoon known as a Yale PhD. His template is essentially Marxist, his tale is tragic, and the problem is capitalism. Paul's stubborn neighbors, he says, were dupes who got suckered into helping great capitalists destroy the land.

These two writers exemplify the two great, contrasting narrative traditions of the Great Plains. Stay with me here, because I am about to impose some academic labels, but they make sense. The two great narrative traditions of the Great Plains are the progressive and the declensionist.

First you have to ignore how both political parties have, over the years, hijacked the word "progressive," and get back to its root, "progress." Progressive storytellers believe we are making progress and are headed toward a brighter future. Sure, there have been difficulties, droughts and plagues and depressions, but those are the things that build character. Enjoy the good times, hold on through the bad times, and have faith in the future.

The other storytelling tradition, the declensionist, is the progressive flipped 180 degrees. The declensionist narrative holds that human experience on the plains is tragic, and it is getting more so all the time. In North Dakota, our resident declensionist was the University of North Dakota historian Elwyn Robinson, with his famous doctrine of the Too-Much Mistake. We must tighten our belts another notch every year, until we just disappear. Leaving not even a smile, but rather a grimace, hanging in the air.

Notice how neatly I have caricatured the two great storytelling traditions of the plains, so that both appear ridiculous? That is what storytellers do. They strip away the details that do not fit, they suppress the evidence that contradicts, and they simplify the narrative for us. This is what the great historians do, and it is what the windbag on the barstool next to you does, too.

The narrative lines of the Great Plains are not geological features. Nor are they Holy Writ. We are the ones who write them into the land.

What if we went to work on a better story — you know, one where you do not already know the end of it when you start reading? Will you tell it with me?

⊱──⊰

I must be moving in the wrong circles. Does no one anymore know what a flickertail is?

"Flickertail State" is the unofficial nickname of North Dakota, used today mainly by smart alecks. According to the secretary of state, the legislature in 1953 voted down a bill to make the moniker official.

Until 1930 the athletic teams of the University of North Dakota were known as the Flickertails. After that they were known as the Fighting Sioux, as anyone knows who followed the logo controversy in the state press. Nevertheless, flickertails appear among the crests embossed on the walls of UND's long-time liberal arts building, Merrifield Hall, constructed in 1930. The Vessel Register of the US Navy includes a cargo vessel called *Flickertail State*.

Still, my casual survey of residents of the Peace Garden State (the official nickname), consisting of the single question, "Do you know what a flickertail is?," gets me blank stares or wild guesses from eighty percent of respondents. It is a GOPHER, for Pete's sake. A flickertail gopher, a.k.a. Richardson's ground squirrel, a.k.a. *Spermophilus richardsonii*, a.k.a. picket pin (for its habit of stretching upright to look around).

Earlier generations on the northern plains did not need to be told what a flickertail was. It figures in the literary works of such authors as Lois Hudson, Wallace Stegner, and W. O. Mitchell, and in the memoirs of Lawrence Welk, who said he earned the money to buy his first accordion from gopher tail bounties. More to the point, the creature haunts the memories of old farm kids across the plains states and prairie provinces.

The greatest memory artist of the plains, William Kurelek of Manitoba, did a wonderfully documentary painting of kids and dogs pursuing gophers, a painting that represents fairly the memories of prairie generations.

Nowadays, though, you can drive across North Dakota in June and not see a single flickertail. There are places in the states and more places in the provinces where they remain common, including many urban environments, where the gophers revive their old reputation as an agricultural pest by mowing down flower plantings and pocking athletic fields.

Memories about gophers are mainly concerned, of course, with killing them. The states and provinces levied bounties for gopher tails, a method of control that perhaps kept the pest numbers down and certainly provided needed pocket change for farm kids. Indeed, one woman in central North Dakota told me she made enough money off gopher tails to buy her father a disk harrow.

This business of gopher hunting is something I have researched — I mean, studied in depth, archives and all — across the prairie provinces, but not in the states. I found that the most complaints of gopher damage to crops came during times when farm conditions created optimal conditions for the animals — the pioneer period, when crops first appeared in the grasslands, and the 1930s, when field abandonment gave plenty of habitat back to the gophers. These also were the times when people most needed the income of bounty money.

In 1921, according to the reports of the Alberta Department of Agriculture, the schoolchildren of that province turned in 2.3 million gopher tails to their teachers. They snared them (the gophers that is) with twine, shot them with .22s (not exactly cost-effective), trapped them, and most of all, pursued them with buckets of water and dogs.

These days I try not even to run over them on the road. And I always say "Flickertail State," never "Peace Garden State." Give my flickertails a chance, and see how long your Peace Garden lasts. But how have we come to the place where I have to explain to native sons and daughters what a flickertail is?

⊱┄◈┄○┄◈┄⊰

We do not live in a classical age, and so we do not speak in iambic pentameter (although I could do so if called upon). Every age, every place has its customary modes of expression. One of ours, here and now, is the rant. This literary form thrives on the internet, especially in anonymous sectors of that virtual world. A rant is a litany of denunciations and indignations spoken to let off steam.

The form broke through into national advertising in Canada a few years ago with a Molson beer commercial featuring a young man speaking a piece known simply as "The Rant" — a catalog of resentments dealing with American misunderstandings of Canada. Unfortunately, the young fellow who delivered The Rant so passionately has since moved to the states.

About the time George W. Bush took office as president I began receiving copies of a rant entitled, "Brushing Up on Southern Manners." This was a list of cautions to "ALL visiting Northerners And Northeastern Urbanites" as to their behavior when visiting the South. Every caution closed with a warning something like, "or we will have to kick your —."

Now, that sort of rhetoric might seem unlikely on the northern plains, but remember it was mild-mannered Canadians who made The Rant into an icon of popular culture. Sure enough, in subsequent weeks I received no less than eight copies of a rant, adapted from the southern version, purporting to have been "Issued by the North Dakota Tourism Bureau to ALL visiting Californians and Northeastern Urbanites" and closing with the ironic benediction, "Enjoy your visit in the Peace Garden State!"

All versions are profane, but some tone down the usage in the style of Sarge in a Beetle Bailey cartoon, a pattern I will follow here in the interest of decency. I call this document the North Dakota Rant. It admonishes us, among other things, thus:

- Don't order filet mignon or pasta primavera at Kroll's Kitchen. It's a diner. They serve breakfast 24 hours a day. Let them cook something they know. If you upset the ladies in the kitchen, they'll kick your @$%. [Clearly, the author of this rant has been watching those Kroll's commercials on TV.]

- Don't laugh at the names of our little towns (Minnewauken, Rolla, Gackle, Osnabrock, Cando, Walhalla, Zap, etc.) or we will just HAVE to kick your @$%.

- We have plenty of business sense. You have to make a living up here. Naturally, we do sometimes have small lapses in judgment from time to time, but we are not dumb enough to let someone move to our state in order to run for the Senate. If someone tried to do that, we would kick their @$%.

- Don't laugh at our giant fiberglass cows and our turtles made out of car parts. Anything that inspires tourists to buy 50,000 postcards can't be bad. When you're in Jamestown, don't point at the **&!# on the giant buffalo or we'll kick your @$%.

- We are fully aware of how cold it gets here in the winter, so shut the %&! up. Just spend your money and get the %&! out of here or we'll kick your @$%.

- Don't complain that North Dakota is flat and that there aren't enough trees. If you whine about OUR scenic beauty we'll kick your @$% all the way back to Cleveland.

- Last, but not least, DO NOT DARE to come out here and tell us how the prairie should "go back to the buffalo." This will get your @$% shot (right after it is kicked). Just mention this once and you will go home in a pine box. Minus your @$%.

I will admit that I laughed at the North Dakota Rant. It gives me no comfort, however.

▷┄◈┄○┄◁┄◁

E very year it appears, mysterious as to origins, no authorship or credit given. It is the Farmers Union Camp Songbook, the official catalog of songs to be sung by Farmers Union youth campers. I have a new copy courtesy of my friend Jared, a camp counselor. I do not know if he can sing a note, he never has around me, but he brought me the songbook.

The repertoire of Farmers Union summer campers is nothing if not eclectic. It includes "Puff the Magic Dragon," "Jeremiah Was a Bullfrog," and "God Bless My Underwear"—you know how it goes—

> God bless my underwear,
>
> My only pair.
>
> Stand beside them and guide them,
>
> As they sit in a heap by the chair.

There are old standards of farm activism, too. Right up front we find that favorite from the Populist days of the 1890s, "The Farmer Is the Man."

> When the banker says he's broke,
>
> And the merchant's up in smoke,
>
> They forget that it's the farmer feeds them all.
>
> It would put them to the test
>
> If the farmer took a rest,
>
> Because the farmer is the man who feeds them all.

When I studied agricultural economics in college, that was what we called farm fundamentalism.

Some songs, too, partake of heartfelt love of the land, this land, this place on the prairies. For instance, some years ago a woman from South Dakota taught me how to sing one song in the book.

As I recall, it goes like this.

> I love the mountains, I love the hills,
> Winding rivers and whispering rills.
> But my heart with contentment fills,
> Out on the plains I love.
> Out on the plains where the wind blows free,
> That is the place I am longing to be.
> There good fortune will smile on me,
> There let me live and die.
> On me the city casts no spells.
> I hate its noise and assorted smells.
> Oh, what relief when my road map tells
> I'm on the plains again.
> If you would live where the skies are blue,
> North Dakota's the land for you.
> Land where people are brave and true –
> This is the land we love.
> Misty moon in the autumn sky,
> Listening to the wild goose cry.
> Sometimes I wish that I might fly
> Back to Dakota's plains.
> Out on the plains where the wind blows free,
> That is the place I am longing to be.
> There good fortune will smile on me,
> There let me live and die.

Later I learned these stanzas were penned by the Icelandic sage, Snorri Thorfinnson. Now we are getting somewhere. The plains I love.

⊷•◦•⊶

Eric Sevareid, revered commentator on CBS News, favorite son of Velva, North Dakota, has been the subject of quite a bit of my reading. You might think there is not much new to say about such a celebrated figure, but to the contrary, there is plenty of fresh material to take up.

For instance, I ordered microfilm of the *Velva Journal* to study a little-known guest column written by Sevareid for the old home-town paper. This was the situation. In June 1933 Bud Sevareid had begun both his student career at the University of Minnesota and his journalistic career in Minneapolis. He decided to take some time off and work in a gold mine in California. This meant riding the rails west, with a stopover in Velva. Sevareid wrote a humorous column about his visit that was published on July 13, 1933. It begins like this:

> When I left Velva at the age of 12, this, I dreamed, would be my return:
>
> In a suit of Panama white (to match my limousine) I would roll into town in a cloud of dust. At my leisurely command, the uniformed chauffeur would twist to a stop before McKnight's. Then, a twenty-five cent cigar jutting from my handsome, world-weary mouth, I would step from the car, into the store, calmly order 800 ice cream cones, and distribute them to the crowd of gaping little boys and girls. And I would smile politely at the whispered remarks, such as: "I always knew that Sevareid boy would make good."

This, according to Sevareid, is how things really happened.

> Sunburned and blistered, skin on my nose peeling like curled wallpaper, my left shank gone bad, I backed my painful way into Main street with a soiled pack sack sagging from my two-by-four shoulders. And the first remark my burning ears caught was: "My gosh, who is that funny looking oaf?"

I do not know about you, but I never had fantasies about a homecoming to the acclaim of the folks back in the old hometown. It is more my desire to slip in and out quietly, preferably with a little time spent in my old duck blind.

Sevareid's scenario, I would say, is the work of a young man who has aspirations, expects to be a big man someday, but does not yet take himself that seriously. He cares about what people in Velva think, though.

He particularly cares about one citizen of Velva, the girl of his dreams, Helen Bloomquist. According to Sevareid's biographer, the young man was interested in looking her up, and he found her at the reunion dance that happened to be taking place that night. Stealing the final dance with the fair Helen, Bud was disappointed to learn she was married — and not even to his old rival, Walter Wilson, but rather to another chap, John Kramer. Of this episode Sevareid writes,

> The annual high school homecoming was but a few hours away when I arrived. Donald Dickinson, high pressure spokesman of the event, thought he would capitalize on my return (the optimist). "Bud Sevareid will be there," he told prospective homecomers.

To which synopsis the editor of the *Journal*, Bill Francis, added this note: "The reunion was attended by an exceptionally small number this year."

I will note just two things more about what Sevareid wrote about his 1933 homecoming. First, he inventoried the things that had changed, and the things that had stayed the same. Change and constancy were important things to Sevareid. Second, Bud Sevareid showed he had learned some journalistic lessons by hanging around the office of the *Journal*. If you want to make friends and sell papers, you need to mention a lot of people by name and affirm them in print. The affirmation sometimes is in the form of gentle mockery, because in the rhetoric of the prairies, joshing is a way of expressing affection.

"The cutest thing in town," writes Sevareid: "Mrs. James Motley's youngest."

"Most beautiful thing in North Dakota," he prompts: "The drive from Minot to Velva."

"Most notable addition to Velva: Marvin Nurnberger's mustache."

And here is the young reporter's closing:

> It was surprising to find the shaky wooden bridge over the river at the park, still upright. But not surprising to find the sign it bears, "Welcome to Velva," still in existence and still full of meaning.

Many Americans have read Sevareid's memoir, *Not So Wild a Dream*, which contains substantial remarks about Velva and North Dakota, then carries the story on through his life as a World War II correspondent and a CBS commentator. Far fewer have read his remarks of 1933, the first time the adult reporter returned to his boyhood home, which I just discussed.

Now I turn to the most significant of all Sevareid's writings about Velva and North Dakota—his 1956 article for *Collier's* magazine entitled, "You Can Go Home Again." This essay is his most direct and thoughtful confrontation with his prairie past, and it deserves direct and thoughtful consideration.

Alighting in Minot on the *Empire Builder*, Sevareid makes the drive to Velva in a rented Studebaker. A middle-aged man is coming home to settle something, that thing being his relationship, if there is one, with his boyhood home. Sevareid is roasting that old familiar chestnut, the identity question. "Where are we here on the cold, flat top of our country?" he asks. "What am I doing here?"

Sevareid prowls around the town, noting again all the things that have changed, as well as those that have remained the same. He stays with Bill Francis, former editor of the *Velva Journal*, and his wife, the former Mrs. Beebe, whom he had known as "Aunt Jesse." He chats with Oscar and Gertrude Anderson, who are retired from running their business and living comfortably. Oscar is truly vested here in Velva, leader of all sorts of community activities, and just the year previous published a history of the town.

Most affecting for Sevareid, there is another reunion with the beautiful Helen Bloomquist (now Kramer), the girl of his dreams, who introduces her husband and children. He writes of Helen, "She had stayed and she was happy, as she had been fashioned from childhood always to be." (At a Sevareid symposium in Bismarck I met Helen's son Mike, who handed me a framed photograph of his mother at about the age Sevareid would have known her in Velva. She was indeed a memorable beauty.)

Sevareid stumbles along the Mouse riverbank and tastes the tangy skin of a red haw. Finally, crossing the North Bridge, he gives in to his senses and sentiments. "I understood then why I had loved it so and loved its memory always," he writes; "it was, simply, home."

These prairie memoirists such as Sevareid, no matter their sentiments about the old home town, are determined to make something of their childhood experiences. Sevareid, in somewhat self-centered fashion, concludes that the significance of country towns like Velva to the greater world is that they produce and export such men as he. "That is what my home town and yours really are in the American story and system," he writes; "not stagnant plants at all, but seedbeds, ceaselessly renewing the nation . . . pulsating with the lives that come to them and the lives they give away."

This statement strikes me as rather colonialist. I would like to think that the communities of the plains have aspirations and destinies of their own, and are not mere brooder houses for the benefit of other, supposedly more important places. I am not sure we should let expatriate memoirists such as Sevareid, who have their personal agendas, tell the story of Velva. Who should tell the story, then? I vote for Oscar Anderson. I wish Sevareid had taken a little time to find out about Velva from the guy who knew its history.

›‐┼◦┼›‐○‐‹┼◦┼‹

After a lapse of years we returned to the little town of Eastend, Saskatchewan, boyhood home of Wallace Stegner, winner of the Pulitzer Prize and the National Book Award. This place is the subject of Stegner's celebrated memoir, *Wolf Willow*. We sometimes forget that it also is the home of six-hundred-and-some people, all of whom have their own stories to tell.

Stegner as a lad experienced the hurley-burley and the optimistic ozone of the frontier days of the 1910s. A generation later he returned to the old home town, did some research, collected his memories, wrote his book, and closed it with a chapter called "False Front Athens." Here he assesses whether Eastend (called Whitemud in his book) has lived up to its promise.

In a word — No. In a passage famous for its acidity, Stegner writes, "Dead, dead, dead says the mind contemplating the town's life. . . . A dull, dull little town where nothing passes but the wind." In particular, he concludes that no one of intellectual bent could live there. He makes certain exceptions for the local historian, Corky Jones, and the blacksmith, Jack Wilkinson, who built his own astronomical observatory.

So, still another generation passes, and here we come to Eastend, Stegner's home town, in many ways everybody's home town on the plains, and we think about what he wrote. Like him, too, we nose around and talk to people.

We think Stegner was unduly harsh. In the first place, Corky Jones and Jack Wilkinson were even more remarkable individuals than Stegner told us. Reading writings by Jones, I reckon he was not just a happy amateur, but a serious thinker about local history. Moreover, his pioneering work in paleontology has earned the respect of modern professionals. Jack Wilkinson not only built a telescope in his blacksmith shop but also gathered around him a regular club of working machinists who would wheel it out into the starry night and take turns contemplating the universe.

When Wilkinson died, an astronomy club formed to preserve and operate his equipment. In Eastend we spent a lovely evening with Sig and Deb Giverhaug, who, after a lapse of years, have revived the astronomy club again. We also met other people who were making art, discussing books, and investigating their history in Eastend.

Our view of the intellectual community of Eastend broadened when we spent an afternoon in the museum. One exhibit after another showed the work of citizens who were building airplanes, collecting artifacts and fossils, making music, and in other ways engaging in the life of the mind. Not to over-romanticize this — it is not a town of philosopher kings — but Eastend has never been dead.

Which still brings us back to Stegner's question of whether a real intellectual — such as he — could live in such a town. The answer is not categorical. Could an intellectual live in a prairie town? Of course. Could Wallace Stegner — with his bag of boyhood and adult experiences — live in Eastend? No. And that has to do both with Eastend and with him.

⊷―⊶―○―⊷―⊶

Charlie's Lunch is an establishment pretty much unknown outside of Eastend, Saskatchewan — a town of six hundred people where the Pulitzer Prize-winning author, Wallace Stegner, happened to spend much of his boyhood. Stegner tells us nothing about Charles Goulet and his little café, nor will you find it in any tourist guides.

Oilfield workers have discovered Charlie's, though, and they crowd in between the regular coffee klatches and wolf the sloppy hamburgers set out by the able woman currently in charge, Sheri Kohl. Charlie, whom I met years ago, has passed away, and is now a man of legend: people love to tell stories about his cranky dispo-

Charlie's Lunch, a reservoir of community in Eastend, Saskatchewan

sition and his community spirit. The annual community Christmas celebration is still known as Charlie's Christmas.

Sometimes the reservoir of community in a prairie town pools into in an odd place, such as Charlie's Lunch. Across the street is Jack's Café, celebrated across the country for Greek and Canadian cuisine. Up the street is the imposing Cypress Hotel, come back to life as a dining establishment since the owners imported a crew of Filipino immigrants to provide reliable staffing. Still, if you want to meet people and take a community pulse, you go to Charlie's.

Which is where we became acquainted, over coffee, with Bev and Sig Giverhaug. They are citizens of Eastend, and they are astronomers. This is to say, they have taken charge of the Wilkinson Memorial Observatory on the hilltop just southwest of town.

There they introduce visitors young and old to the wonders of the universe.

What the heck is an observatory doing in this little prairie town? That goes back to the blacksmith Jack Wilkinson, a handy and curious fellow who in the 1940s built himself a 10-cm refractor telescope, and after that a 15-cm reflector. I really mean he built these devices himself, right down to grinding the mirror over the winter at home.

All well and good, but maybe this guy Wilkinson was just a curious crank with a little talent. Well, no — he got the local pharmacist and the jeweler involved for coating the mirror, too. Then he got a bunch of other machinists from Eastend and surrounding villages to help out. They salvaged metal from a crashed aircraft to make a stable frame, designed and built an equatorial mount so as to track stars in line with the earth's rotation, and brought in a new 20-cm telescope.

The frame was mounted on a set of rollers, so on promising nights for celestial observation, all these machinists would wheel the telescope out of Jack's workshop onto the sidewalk and stay up through the night contemplating the heavens. They were just working guys in a dusty prairie village, but they sought the things which are above.

The way Wallace Stegner describes Eastend, it was a place without much sense of community and hardly any intellectual activity. Perhaps he needed to spend a little time with Charlie and Jack. There is a time to drink coffee, and a time to contemplate the stars.

9. EPILOGUE

William Stafford and Wallace Stegner died in the same year, 1993. Born in 1952, I came along a little after them, grew up with an understanding of the things they wrote about, but now linger after they are gone, hanging in here on the Great Plains, observing and thinking as the land and people continue the long spin dance of prairie life. I am struggling for the right metaphor here, and finally settling on burial. A decent burial, with all due honors. Moving on with the cycle of life, and of lives.

We of the northern plains have ways of thinking we have canonized over a long generation of regional life. The prophet of these times, here in North Dakota, was a scholar named Elwyn Robinson. Now I wish to preach over this great man.

Elwyn Robinson, a native of Ohio educated at Oberlin College and Case Western Reserve University, came to Grand Forks in 1935. He taught history at the University of North Dakota until his retirement in 1974 and died in 1985. He began a cultivated interest in the history of North Dakota with the retirement in 1944 of Orin G. Libby, the founding father of North Dakota history, and soon would eclipse the old master in the interpretation of his adopted state.

Robinson told us what to think about this place. In 1958 he laid out his famous "Six Themes" of North Dakota history. He would incorporate the same ideas into his magisterial *History of North Dakota*, published in 1966. Sure, professors publish lots of books and articles, and so what, but you have to remember Robinson also taught these ideas to a whole generation of our best and brightest going through the university. Our political leaders, our business elite, our newspaper editors took careful notes and drilled themselves on Robinson's principles. We were imprinted.

I want to emphasize that Robinson's ideas were insightful, they were right, they were prophetic. He told us what we needed to know in 1960. He served us well. He told us we lived in a land of disadvantage. We were remote from centers of economic power, a colonial hinterland whose people often turned to radical solutions in the struggle against distant and exploitive powers.

We lived in a hard country that reminded us every day — or at least, with every blizzard or drought — of the limitations of life in a semiarid land. In our settlement generation we committed the Too-Much Mistake, building too many railroads, grain elevators, towns, schools, churches, Optimist clubs — too many of everything. Now it was time, Robinson said, to make the painful and long-overdue adjustments to life in a semiarid hinterland. The message was, tighten our belts and learn to live with less.

This was a hard teaching. Most of us cleared out for Minneapolis or Seattle or Lodi. The rest of us, chastened, began our penance. In an odd way, you see, there was comfort in Robinson's teaching. It said we were not to blame. We were paying for mistakes of the past. The standard regional joke became, "Will the last one to leave please turn out the lights?" Oh, we were good, frugal folk.

A generation hence, we still are. The teachings of Elwyn Robinson got us through the long night of regional life. Because we have so canonized them, however, we may not be well-prepared for life in our own times. The unintended result of Robinson's teaching — our fault, not his — is that it left us with a generation of leaders who defined statesmanship as the orderly dismantlement of our civilization.

In a world of digital communications and containerized transport, there no longer is such a thing as a hinterland. We still live in a semiarid country, but even when agriculture fails, we run budget surpluses. We no longer are necessarily and directly tied to the land as agriculturalists. As a resource state, we enjoy overwhelming advantages in the new world economy.

So let us praise Elwyn Robinson. And then let us do him the honor of emulating him — of looking about us, seeing things as they are, and telling new stories that will serve the next generation as well as he served the one previous.

This, too, is a hard teaching. It removes the fate of our home country from the realm of determinisms and places it into the realm of contingencies. We do not know just what is coming up the pike, but it will be up to us — not some higher power or disembodied force — to deal with it.

A great poet of my own generation on the plains, Timothy Murphy, spoke for us in *Set the Ploughshare Deep*, just as the twentieth century gave way to the twenty-first.

> The steeples are toppled
> and the land unpeopled,
> reclaimed by thistle
> and buffalo grass.

We were, you see, a tragic generation on the plains, false-fronted, too-much-mistaken, dispossessed on a cold, flat top of a country. What remained for us was to finish our part in a morality play. We were, as Tim wrote,

> learning how to die
> with our feet stuck in the muck
> and our eyes trained on the sky.

I suspect that most people who knew Tim in 2000 would be surprised he is still alive today. He is, in fact, at the height of his powers, writing his fool head off. His generational peer, I find myself writing more, and accomplishing more, than in any other period of my life.

It would be presumptuous to pose Tim and me as metaphors for the renewal of our home country. Still, I have said, with Stafford, "My self will be the plain."

—————

A couple thousand times since 1983 I have opened a screen to compose an essay under the title, "Plains Folk." I am thankful to the readers and listeners who have sustained the enterprise. I would like to talk with you a little now as fellow people of the plains. Those of you unfortunate enough to live in forested regions, do the best you can.

Some of us feel called to preach the gospel of the regional project, to talk and talk about the circumstances and features and aspirations of regional life. There is a need, I hope, for a few such prophets, but only, I suspect, a few. Too much of this sort of exhortation can be tedious. For the mass of us, it is more important to walk the walk than to talk the talk. What I mean by this is, just settle in and live the good life on the Great Plains of North America.

In fact I have a folder I keep adding notes to that carries the title, "On the Level: Living the Good Life on the North American Plains." Someday I will write up all the pearls of wisdom therein, I am not sure when, because I am still practicing what I intend to preach. I can give you an update, though. I will put this in the form of four adjectives that I think describe the good life on the plains.

First, the good life on the plains is sensate. I got this adjective from Father Taras Miles of St. Demetrius Ukrainian Catholic Church, Billings County, as we came in for Mass. He knew it would

Fr. Taras Miles walks Dr. Suzzanne Kelley into St. Demetrius Ukrainian Catholic Church, Billings County, North Dakota

be long, and for us, often incomprehensible, so he advised us to enjoy the Mass as a "sensate experience."

There is an alternative trope about regional life often propounded, both in folk saying and in serious literature — the idea that life on the plains is ascetic, even hard, a narrative of deprivation that makes us better people in the end. This is not my logic of life on the plains, for it is the concrete experiences of the senses that ground the intellectual sense of place and fill our lives. Living here, you need to make space for such experiences. For me, this means things like sharp-tailed grouse hunting, snowshoeing, and juneberries.

Second, the good life on the plains is literate. While preparing this manuscript, I read a biography of John Joseph Mathews, the Osage author. In particular I relished reading of his interactions with others of the literary community in mid-twentieth century: the legendary editor, Savoie Lottinville; the folklorist, J. Frank Dobie; the Osage Rhodes scholar, Carter Revard. I suppose I read a lot, generally three books at the same time.

Being literate in the way I am talking about here, however, is not just reading books and knowing authors. What I want to establish is the value of knowledge and reflection. The prairie landscape and everything therein is more meaningful, and more conducive to contentment, if you have reference points — historical, poetic, geological, ecological.

Third, the good life is social. This is the one I need most to work on. At our house, we tend to get so immersed in work, and sometimes play, that social networks suffer. This resonates with the social experience of my entire generation on the plains, as communities atrophied due to demographic and economic decline. With the disappearance of the old rural culture on the plains, we should pay thoughtful attention to the construction, or perhaps just the emergence, of social ties for the twenty-first century.

Fourth, by way of adjectives — the good life on the plains is situational. I need a better adjective to describe what I am talking about. I mean coming to recognize the prairies as your default comfort landscape. I have the advantage here. Wide open spaces are my comfort zone. The Minnesota lake country holds no attraction. Oceans make me uncomfortable. Prairie, like the comfortably mixed countryside of the Missouri Coteau, is the Middle Landscape for me.

When we meet, therefore, let us talk of the regional project, of the sense of place, of splendid landscapes, and of sublime literary passages. Let us also speak of stories, juneberries, retrieving dogs, friends, farms, pies, and grandchildren.

Retired? Not hardly. Just living well.

INDEX

ABOUT THE AUTHOR

Thomas D. (Tom) Isern is professor of history & University Distinguished Professor, North Dakota State University. His academic specialty is the history and folklore of the Great Plains of North America, his research and teaching comprising both the American plains and the Canadian prairies. He is the author or co-author of six books, including *Dakota Circle: Excursions on the True Plains*, published by the Institute for Regional Studies (forerunner of North Dakota State University Press).

Isern is best known within the region of the northern plains as the author of *Plains Folk*, the radio feature he reads weekly to a statewide audience on Prairie Public.

A native of western Kansas, he holds a BA degree from Bethany College as well as MA and PhD degrees from Oklahoma State University. Prior to coming to NDSU in 1992, he served eleven years on the faculty of Emporia State University, Kansas.

Isern is married to historian and publisher Suzanne Kelley. They happily boast of four adult children and eight grandchildren and shamelessly dote upon a beagle and a Labrador retriever. Together, too, they share offshore research interests in New Zealand and Australia.

ABOUT THE PRESS

North Dakota State University Press (NDSU Press) exists to stimulate and coordinate interdisciplinary regional scholarship. These regions include the Red River Valley, the state of North Dakota, the plains of North America (comprising both the Great Plains of the United States and the prairies of Canada), and comparable regions of other continents. We publish peer reviewed regional scholarship shaped by national and international events and comparative studies.

Neither topic nor discipline limits the scope of NDSU Press publications. We consider manuscripts in any field of learning. We define our scope, however, by a regional focus in accord with the press's mission. Generally, works published by NDSU Press address regional life directly, as the subject of study. Such works contribute to scholarly knowledge of region (that is, discovery of new knowledge) or to public consciousness of region (that is, dissemination of information, or interpretation of regional experience). Where regions abroad are treated, either for comparison or because of ties to those North American regions of primary concern to the press, the linkages are made plain. For nearly three-quarters of a century, NDSU Press has published substantial trade books, but the line of publications is not limited to that genre. We also publish textbooks (at any level), reference books, anthologies, reprints, papers, proceedings, and monographs. The press also considers works of poetry or fiction, provided they are established regional classics or they promise to assume landmark or reference status for the region. We select biographical or autobiographical works carefully for their prospective contribution to regional knowledge and culture. All publications, in whatever genre, are of such quality and substance as to embellish the imprint of NDSU Press.

We changed our imprint to North Dakota State University Press in January 2016. Prior to that, and since 1950, we published as the North Dakota Institute for Regional Studies Press. We continue to operate under the umbrella of the North Dakota Institute for Regional Studies, located at North Dakota State University.